# Problem Solving to Improve Classroom Learning

RICHARD SCHMUCK
MARK CHESLER
RONALD LIPPITT
*Center for Research on Utilization of Scientific Knowledge*
*Institute for Social Research*
*University of Michigan*

*74122*

Science Research Associates, Inc.   Chicago

A Subsidiary of IBM

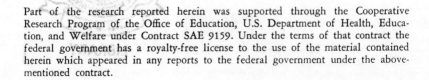

Part of the research reported herein was supported through the Cooperative Research Program of the Office of Education, U.S. Department of Health, Education, and Welfare under Contract SAE 9159. Under the terms of that contract the federal government has a royalty-free license to the use of the material contained herein which appeared in any reports to the federal government under the above-mentioned contract.

# PREFACE

The teacher who wants to keep abreast of new knowledge in the behavioral sciences and utilize it to improve his teaching techniques and professional effectiveness faces a formidable challenge. Fortunately this challenge is not solely the teacher's responsibility. Scientists from the various disciplines are seeking ways of collaborating with educational specialists to apply developments in the behavioral sciences to the classroom and to improve channels of communication to teachers.

*Problem Solving to Improve Classroom Learning* is one of the three TEACHER RESOURCE BOOKLETS ON CLASSROOM SOCIAL RELATIONS AND LEARNING that grew out of such a cooperative research effort. At the Center for Research on Utilization of Scientific Knowledge at the University of Michigan, a team of social scientists and educational specialists for over a decade has been exploring some of the possibilities for cooperative research in the behavioral sciences and the application of the results of such research to the classroom. The projects have been supported by the U.S. Office of Education,* the National Institute of Mental Health,† and the McGregor Foundation.

The relation between classroom interpersonal relations and the effective learning of subject matter has been investigated through research questions such as these: What effect does the social power or social acceptance possessed or lacked by students have on their learning? What are the dynamics that make it difficult for a socially ineffective child to improve his status in the group? What kind of perceptions and expectations do teachers and students have of one another? What are the effects of children of different ages learning together? How can the socially ineffective child be helped to use his learning potential better?

Data have been gathered from several hundred classrooms through the use of diagnostic tools dealing with classroom social structures, individual and group attitudes toward learning, significant environmental forces influencing both teachers and students, and the nature of the student-teacher interaction. On the basis of these data the teachers participating in the research projects modified many of the preliminary diagnostic instruments and developed plans for altering their teaching methods to improve the learning climate of the classroom. Much ingenuity was shown by the participating teachers in taking the step from "What do the data say?" to "What can be done in my classroom to improve mental health and learning?" Further data were then gathered, again through the use

---

*OE contract SAE 9159.
†NIMH grants M 919, OM 376, and MH 01780-08.

iii

of diagnostic tools, on the success or failure of the various plans and teaching methods that were developed.

This series of TEACHER RESOURCE BOOKLETS ON CLASSROOM SOCIAL RELATIONS AND LEARNING presents some of the knowledge gained from those studies.

*Problem Solving to Improve Classroom Learning* is the most comprehensive of the three booklets. It describes the whole problem-solving sequence, from perception of classroom difficulties through the evaluation of the remedial action taken. It deals with the issues of identifying problems in classroom life, selecting or developing appropriate diagnostic tools to analyze these problems, using diagnostic data and behavioral science resources to develop a plan for improving the learning atmosphere in the classroom, carrying out planned changes in classroom life, and evaluating the changes. Practical illustrations were provided from the experience of a variety of teachers and students who participated in the research projects.

*Diagnosing Classroom Learning Environments* focuses upon one stage of the problem-solving sequence—the process of getting reliable information about the actual state of affairs in the classroom. It presents and discusses some of the data-gathering instruments and techniques that have proved useful; it also provides suggestions on organizing the data so that the teacher can focus his efforts on changing the classroom learning environment.

*Role-Playing Methods in the Classroom* is about a technique that has proved highly useful to many teachers for dealing with a variety of classroom problems and reaching certain learning objectives. The booklet discusses the theoretical background of role playing and gives a step-by-step discussion of how to use role playing in the classroom. There are sample role-playing situations, suggestions on how to get started, advice on when to be cautious, discussions of the appropriateness of role playing for children of various ages and social-economic backgrounds, and case studies of groups of teachers and students using role playing under a variety of circumstances and for a variety of reasons.

The three booklets were written to complement each other. Since *Problem Solving* describes the whole problem-solving process in the classroom, it would be advantageous to read it first. It will provide an overview of the series and give the general framework of processes and concepts into which the other two booklets fit. However, although it describes a variety of methods designed to improve the classroom learning atmosphere, it does not do so with the extensive discussion and wealth of illustrative material that is focused upon one such method in *Role-Playing Methods*. And although *Role-Playing Methods* describes in detail one method of working with classroom problems, it has no extended treatment of how these problems are discovered, of how data are gathered about the problems, or of how progress is to be measured. For a detailed analysis of problem-discovery and data-gathering techniques, the reader is referred to *Diagnosing Classroom Learning Environments.*

The reader who wants to examine the theories and the research findings on which these three booklets are based is advised to turn to *Understanding Classroom Social Relations and Learning.** The theories that relate classroom interpersonal relations and subject-matter learning are fully elaborated in that book, and the results of ten years of research in the schools to investigate the validity of these theories are presented.

The degree to which the school should be allowed to inquire into the personal and interpersonal life of the student is occasionally questioned. Articles have been written about the dangers of psychological tests, and legislation has been introduced in some states to restrict or prevent teachers and scientists from obtaining and utilizing such information. This matter is of fundamental concern to teachers who would act upon the suggestions in this series of booklets.

The research findings described in *Understanding Classroom Social Relations and Learning* give major support to the desirability of vigorous efforts on the part of the school and the teacher to understand and improve the mental health and learning climate of the classroom. The research has found that the mentally healthy student does learn academic subject matter better. Teachers who can diagnose and improve the learning atmosphere of their classrooms can thereby be better teachers. Accordingly, the teaching profession would be wise to extend its understanding of classroom social procedures and the techniques for dealing with them, while at the same time exercising caution that the use of these techniques is not extended beyond the teacher's competence and the limits of the educational environment.

Unprofessional use of information about students and unwise applications of diagnostic data by teachers can be greatly reduced by better teacher training, by providing more focused and usable diagnostic materials, and by opening the channels of communication between the social scientist and the teacher. The materials in this series of booklets and the research on which they are based are directed toward these goals.

We wish to acknowledge the extensive teamwork that has made these research projects possible. In addition to the coauthors of this booklet, Richard Schmuck, Mark Chesler, and Ronald Lippitt, other senior collaborators in the projects have been Robert Fox, Mabel Kaufman, Margaret Barron Luszki, and Elmer Van Egmond. The secretarial work has been

*Lippitt, Fox, Schmuck, and Van Egmond (Chicago: Science Research Associates, 1966).

led with dedication by Karen Donahue. If it were possible, each classroom teacher, each principal, each interviewer, each statistician, and each social scientist who made his unique contribution would be introduced to the reader by name. That so many should become so highly involved in an effort requiring extensive time beyond the usual demands, and professional skill beyond that normally expected, speaks well of their concern for the ideas presented in this series of booklets. We hope their efforts are rewarded by your finding *Problem Solving to Improve Classroom Learning* truly helpful.

RONALD LIPPITT
ROBERT FOX
*Program Coordinators*

# TABLE OF CONTENTS

# CHAPTER ONE

# Classrooms with Problems

Teaching and learning are complementary acts that involve an interpersonal process between at least two people. When this process takes place in a classroom it is complicated and affected by the many relations among the students, and between the students and the teacher. In some cases the learning process is enhanced by peer relations that actively support a productive learning atmosphere; in other cases the learning process is inhibited by peer relations. The teacher's style and the subject matter, the child's own feeling about himself and his academic abilities, and the nature of the social relations in the classroom all are major influences on this teaching-learning process.

This introductory chapter will show some actual influences complicating the learning process for students. The illustrations were chosen from several classrooms with relatively common problems. These classrooms and their problems will be used again in this booklet to illustrate the phases of a problem-solving sequence designed to help improve classroom conditions that impede the learning process.

First, let us look at a fifth-grade classroom in the lower-middle-class district of a large city. The teacher, Mrs. Monroe, is frustrated because her students do not appear to be making academic progress. Their mastery of the subject matter is not good, and she feels they are performing less competently and effectively than students she has had in the past. Let us look at some interaction that occurred in Mrs. Monroe's classroom on a typical morning.

Mrs. Monroe said, "Will someone volunteer to read the next passage from the book?"

1

One child, Richard, in the back of the room started to raise his hand, hesitated, looked around, and then pulled his hand down again; but Mrs. Monroe saw him and asked him to read. He read falteringly, constantly looking around to see how his peers were reacting. Other children in the class occasionally tittered and squirmed until Mrs. Monroe asked them to be quiet.

Whenever Mrs. Monroe asked for volunteers, the students in general were reluctant to read in front of the class. In this particular instance, the student who started to raise his hand showed ambivalence between the desire to perform and fear of how his classmates would react. When he finally did read, his classmates reacted with ridicule, and he perspired, fidgeted, and performed poorly. In this kind of classroom situation it is difficult for children to volunteer to perform tasks in front of their peers.

Later, another interaction between Mrs. Monroe and Richard occurred.

Mrs. Monroe said, "Well, Richard, I can see you're having trouble figuring out the meaning of this paragraph. Can someone help Richard with the answer? Can someone tell us what the meaning of this paragraph is, and help Richard?"

None of the students responded to her request.

Here is another example of students not volunteering to participate, this time not volunteering to help their peers in academic work. Moreover, Mrs. Monroe noticed not only that the students were unwilling to help one another publicly, but also that when she organized them into small groups to do classwork, or to prepare a presentation for the class, they were still unable to help one another and to work together very well. It is obvious that there were some strong resistances among the students to offering help to one another, and a clear lack of support for children who wanted to take some initiative.

Another excerpt from Mrs. Monroe's classroom may help reveal some of the dynamics of this process.

Mrs. Monroe said, "John, why don't you want to answer my question?" John replied, "Well, I don't know. I don't know the answer." Mrs. Monroe then asked, "Well, John, can you guess at the answer?" John responded, "No, ma'am. I guess I'm just not smart enough."

This sort of interchange occurred often in Mrs. Monroe's classroom. For the most part, the children did not respect their intellectual resources and were not confident of their ability to do the subject-matter work. If we couple this personal lack of confidence with the lack of mutual support and the strong and obvious peer resistance to those who took academic initiative, we can see the operation of a vicious cycle of peer interaction that served to lower the students' respect for their own abilities. Therefore the students made few attempts to take initiative or to perform effectively,

2

and personal evidences of failure further reinforced their hesitancy and sense of incompetence. In such a case a child's ordinary hesitancy is caught up in a cycle of disapproval and rejection of academic tasks that makes the classroom very uncomfortable—and makes it very difficult for the student to actualize his intellectual potentials and perform subject-matter work effectively.

Another example of classroom problems will be taken from a secondary school in a middle-class suburban area. Mrs. Jefferson, teaching a class in English literature, was reading from a play and occasionally discussing her interpretations of the drama. At one point in her reading she noticed that a youngster in the back of the room was passing a note to another. She said, "You two in the back there—what are you doing? Bring that note up to the front of the room." Mrs. Jefferson then read the note aloud to the classroom and chastised the two note passers.

A few days before this incident, when some of the students were reading aloud, Mrs. Jefferson was very clear about giving rewards and praising those who had done a good job, and in punishing with criticism and disapproval those students who were unprepared or had done poorly. Mrs. Jefferson is an example of a "strong" teacher, who dominates the classroom with her teaching style and significantly influences the way students behave toward each other in the classroom.

Mrs. Jefferson found that her students did not appear to be able to take much initiative. When she divided them into work groups, none of the groups seemed to be able to function very well until she had given them instructions. After she gave instructions, some of the groups still just sat talking about other things. Although other groups immediately jumped on the topic she had given them and worked on it for a while, they soon stopped and looked again to her for direction. She became concerned that there were patches both of resistance and of quick obedience to her authority throughout the class. Some students appeared highly involved, while others were apathetic. Moreover, she found that whenever she left the classroom, the class became disorderly. Also, whenever a substitute teacher came to teach, it was very difficult for the new teacher to get the class to respond in any orderly and open manner.

These are often the results obtained by a teacher who plays a dominant role, making herself the center of attention in the teaching-learning process—a classroom situation that indeed appeals to some students but does not appeal to others. Mrs. Jefferson's students were dependent on her for structured guidance. When a new teacher who was less authoritarian came to the room, the students failed to respond properly. Mrs. Jefferson's presence was required for classroom order.

Finally, the third classroom that will be described is Mr. Jackson's junior high school class in a working-class suburb. The neighborhood

3

served by this junior high school was changing from all-white middle class to partly Negro. The Negro enrollment in the school had risen from about 1 percent to 25 percent of the student body. Mr. Jackson's class had about twenty Negro students, and it was his observation that the whole class did not work well together. For instance, when he allowed them the freedom to form their own work groups, the Negro and the white students grouped with members of their own races; there were few groups in which members of both races were present. Furthermore, when he asked a Negro student to lead the class or teach a lesson to the class, that youngster seldom called upon a white child to respond to a question; the reverse was also true.

Here is part of a conference Mr. Jackson had with one of his white students after such an occurrence: Mr. Jackson said, "Susan, when you were leading the class I noticed several of the Negro students raised their hands to answer your question, but you didn't call upon them. Can you tell me why?" Susan replied, "Well, I didn't know what they were going to say. I didn't know if they were going to answer the question the way I wanted them to."

On other occasions when a Negro youngster was teaching the class, Mr. Jackson asked the class why few of them volunteered to answer questions. He received no helpful responses. Often he saw members of the class fighting, and these tumultuous and turbulent incidents often occurred between members of the two races. When he stopped them and asked them why they were fighting, every once in a while a clear racial cause was revealed.

For instance, the following discussion occurred after a fight between two of Mr. Jackson's students.

Mr. Jackson said, "Betty Ann, why were you fighting with Susan?"

Betty Ann answered, "Well, Susan called me a black witch."

Mr. Jackson then asked, "Susan, did you call Betty Ann a black witch?"

Susan replied, "Yes, but I didn't mean anything like that by it. I meant that she was just really mean and nasty."

Betty Ann retorted, "Well, I don't like this black witch stuff."

Mr. Jackson said, "Do you think that you two can get along?"

Susan said "Yes," but Betty Ann began to cry as she answered "No!"

Mr. Jackson's class reflects some of the racial tensions of the community. Students are carrying their racial identities into the classroom, and are unable to work productively on academic learning in cross-race and perhaps cross-social-class relations. In addition, the students display a good deal of hostility and aggression in this classroom; the resulting tension most likely seriously diminishes the amount of energy that the students can put into intellectual tasks.

The three classrooms show a wide variety of interpersonal and inter-cultural problems of peers and teachers that undoubtedly affect students' motivation, self-esteem, comfort in the class, and other characteristics related to effective academic learning. These problems are not atypical; they exist in many classrooms in our schools today. In one teacher's class-room these problems may be overt; in another, they may be subtle and difficult to detect. However, inasmuch as teaching is an interpersonal process, involving the teacher and the learner, and the learner is one of a group of learners, the teacher cannot ignore these relationship problems. They make a difference in the way children learn, and teachers who wish to enhance learning and academic motivation must try to solve some of the problems of social relations in their classroom.

CHAPTER TWO

# The Problem-Solving Sequence

Teachers are constantly making decisions about their students. More-over, since students are always changing, the relations between students and teachers are always in flux. Teachers deal with these ever changing conditions and needs in various ways, many of which are inadequate to meet the complexity of classroom phenomena.

Faced with a classroom problem, teachers may deny its existence either consciously or unconsciously. Sometimes teachers fall into this pattern of denial when they lack energy or insight to look beneath the surface appearances of the classroom. *Problem denial* leads to greater leisure and comfort for the teacher and often is used to justify a relaxed approach to the classroom.

Another style of approaching classroom problems is that of the teacher who seeks an unequivocal or dogmatic mandate from an *authority*. The authority can be a person of high prestige and status, a tradition, a moral code, or a set of customs. The teacher's appeal to such authority may take the form of saying, "The professor says this is the way to do it, so no questions need to be asked," or "My colleagues do it this way; it's always been done like this." The teacher's uncritical acceptance of an authority to solve problems in the classroom is usually provoked by the need for personal acceptance or membership in a group of colleagues and a desire for security and conformity.

A third problem-solving style, the *least-effort* style, uses comfort and ease as the determinants of and guides to effective teaching. The teacher with this approach minimizes the amount of energy or time he must spend with problems. "It's just a little problem and easily fixed" and "I don't have the time to spend really working on this" are examples of this style. Resources are explored only if they can be used easily.

Closely related to the low-effort style is one in which the teacher uses his *personal satisfaction* as his main criterion. Information is gathered purely on the basis of how it corresponds to his desires. The teacher projects his desires and his own interpersonal problems onto the students and their interpersonal problems, then proceeds to interpret classroom relations in terms of these projections of self. The arbiter of truth or information is the self, and anything that might disconfirm self or self's desires is rejected. Personal gratification and confirmation of self-esteem are the major needs of a teacher who uses this approach.

The teacher who uses a *pure empiricist* style bases his information and judgments only on the evidence of his senses. The hard physical input of the senses can indeed be discriminately solicited and systematically studied. But the pure form of the empirical method uses only the incoming data as the basis for problem solving, and all deductive or intuitive operations are considered inappropriate. There is distrust of the internal cognitive processes and consequently a great concern to get a vast amount of minute and precise quantification of the classroom's events and inputs. No attention is paid to feelings and subjective attitudes of students or teachers; performance observations take priority. The quantitative information alone is supposed to describe the classroom situation.

The *intuitive* problem-solving style gives priority to thought processes and reason. No empirical testing is necessary in the pure form of this approach; a priori assumption, deductive speculation, and internal logic point the way to solutions and action. Statements such as "I know, without asking, what my students are thinking all the time" and "The data just can't be right" are examples of this style. The appeal to internal cognitive processes assumes a strict congruity between personal thought and the actual workings of the classroom.

These six problem-solving styles are nonscientific or prescientific in that even the more sophisticated of them only partially avail themselves of the tools, data, methods, and theories of the behavioral sciences.

Another problem-solving style, the *empirical-rational,* utilizes major portions of the empiricist and intuitive approaches; it combines sensory data with rational or theoretical considerations. This approach can start with the collection of empirical data or the retrieval of prior investigations of a specific problem and proceed to a rational and empirical test of the alternatives for action. The aim is similar to that of behavioral science strategies; it constructs and tests reliable hypotheses derived from observable data collected or retrieved about human problems.

This booklet will present a form of the empirical-rational problem-solving process particularly suited to solving problems in the classroom. The process will be divided into a five-phase sequence, and each phase

7

will make maximum use of the resources of the behavioral sciences. Each phase will be considered separately, although practical illustrations and case studies will show how the phases flow into one another in the problem-solving sequence. The behavioral science resources are seen as (*a*) the data and conceptual frameworks derived from research that are particularly useful for understanding the complexity of classroom social interactions; (*b*) diagnostic instruments and observational techniques useful for gathering information on the attitudes and activities of students, and gaining feedback on their reactions to the teacher's methods; and (*c*) behavioral scientists themselves insofar as they can be used as demonstrators, collaborators, and consultants. In the organization of this booklet, these resources will not be discussed separately; rather they will be elaborated upon whenever they are appropriate in the problem-solving sequence. For example, the chapter on problem identification will present certain concepts of group dynamics as they pertain to the classroom, the chapter on diagnosis will discuss diagnostic tools, and the chapter on adaptation and action will discuss how the teacher can make use of consultants.

Although a teacher may question whether a method as elaborate as this is needed, the complexity of classroom problems makes a systematic, scientific approach to their solution necessary. A teacher's style of dealing with classroom problems is determined not only by his personality, experience, insight, and training but also by the reactions his style evokes from his students. Yet, the reactions of students to a teacher's style cannot be understood by analysis of the style alone; the individual student as a member of the classroom group, and as a member of the neighborhood and familial groups as well, is mediating a vast series of inputs, only one of which is his perceptions of the teacher. The desired outcome of all these inputs is appropriate and effective behavior in the classroom. Different personal styles and concerns, and divergent cultural and group overlays, as well as classroom events and strains, all help account for the wide variety of idiosyncratic, and often apparently incompatible, learning and acting styles found in the classroom. In a plural, heterogeneous society these differences are positively valued. But valued or not, their existence poses serious problems for teachers who must try to relate to twenty-five or thirty individuals.

## Phases in the Problem-Solving Process

The five phases of the problem-solving process will be briefly reviewed in this section. A case study in the following section will illustrate the phases as they are integrated in an actual problem-solving attempt. Each of these phases will be treated later in separate chapters.

## Phase 1:  Identifying Classroom Problems

The teacher should be clear about his own goals and values, and the learning potentials in his classroom. Secondly, he should be sensitive to the dynamics of student behavior. He watches for signs of student aggression, underlying hostility, and negative attitudes toward academic work. Furthermore, he is attentive to the friendship patterns in the classroom, the cliques that are influencing student behavior, and the feelings of those students who are excluded from these cliques. He is attentive to the influence his personality and teaching style have on his students, as well as to how their behavior influences his.

With this sensitivity to student behavior, the teacher is prepared to make a preliminary and tentative analysis of the problem, using the concepts of the behavioral sciences as an aid. He might, for example, make some very tentative analyses that his students' low motivation to learn emanates from an inadequate home environment, and that their low self-esteem stems from the unfriendly reactions of their peers. Only after he has made a tentative analysis of the problem and constructed hypotheses can the teacher proceed with more formal diagnostic methods.

## Phase 2:  Diagnosing Classroom Problems

In this phase the teacher attempts to probe beneath the surface of classroom activity. He seeks to verify, refute, or refine his initial understanding of it, to locate the sources of disharmony, to find concealed supportive forces that he may work with. He is seeking detailed and sophisticated knowledge of what is happening in his classroom. If, for example, he knows that educational research has found that poor student self-esteem impedes the learning process, he will want to know to what extent his students have poor self-concepts, and what may be happening in his classroom to reinforce these self-concepts. He will look for specific information and will choose diagnostic tools and techniques that will give him knowledge of specifics. He can use diagnostic instruments and observational techniques developed and tested by researchers and other teachers, or he can develop his own.

The teacher will also want to know to what extent the interaction in his classroom is the product of community and cultural forces that he can only indirectly influence in the classroom. There are some diagnostic techniques that will help him determine this; but he will also have to rely upon his objective knowledge of these forces. Chapter Five will discuss how extraschool cultural conditions influence classroom behavior.

## Phase 3:  Developing a Plan

The teacher can now begin to make a plan to improve the classroom situation. He may, if his diagnosis has been thorough and the problem seems to be relatively simple, formulate a plan himself. However, he may want to consult colleagues and to examine plans used with success by others. Case studies and descriptions of innovative techniques have been written up in educational journals, which the teacher may consult. Chapter Seven presents several such techniques, while the case study at the end of this chapter and those in Chapter Ten, as well as the illustrations throughout the booklet, may help the teacher develop a plan of his own. Educational workshops and conferences are other sources of innovative ideas.

## Phase 4:  Adaptation and Action

After the teacher has decided on a plan, especially if he has derived it from a colleague or from reading and research, he must take care that he adapts it to his particular situation. Adaptation calls upon the teacher to use creative insight. This is a crucial phase in the problem-solving process for three reasons: (1) each teacher has a unique personality and teaching style; (2) student characteristics such as age, social background, and previous school experiences differ from class to class; (3) classroom peer groups differ in their social structures and norms. After the teacher has considered the special adaptations of his plan to his own classroom, he may be wise to try out the plan experimentally. When he is finally putting the plan into operation, he may want the support and advice of an interested colleague who may be able to sit in the classroom as an observer. Another method for developing skill with a new teaching practice is to use a tape recorder, so that the teacher can play back the session when he has the time to reflect upon his actions. By these and other methods, the teacher can work to develop skills in using the new teaching practice.

## Phase 5:  Feedback and Evaluation

There are two aspects to this final phase. The teacher should try to get continuous feedback from his students as to the effects the new teaching practice has upon them; and he should attempt a long-term objective evaluation as to whether or not the new practice has improved the classroom learning climate. A prerequisite to obtaining feedback is an atmosphere in which free communication can flow from students to teacher and vice versa. However, there are special devices that the teacher can use to open the communications atmosphere and stimulate feedback. Again, as with diagnostic tools, he may use devices developed and tested by educational researchers and other teachers, or he may develop his own. Long-term evaluation often involves more systematic measurement. The teacher may use instruments and observational techniques similar to those he used in the diagnosis stage in order to make before-and-after comparisons. He may also want to compare the class in which the new practice was used with one in which he used his old methods.

Classroom problem solving is an unending activity, for until the teacher can say that his students have an optimal learning environment in his classroom, there will still be problems to solve. After an evaluation of the effects of a new teaching practice has been made, the teacher may find that the old problems still remain, although perhaps in an attenuated form, and that he should develop further plans for working on them. Often the solution of one problem will create a situation in which other problems can be seen more clearly and attended to. Occasionally the solution of a major classroom problem of peer relations may release heretofore buried or inhibited energies of ignored and rejected students; and thus new problems are created. The teacher should not be discouraged by this; the capacity for personal growth can be viewed as the ability to solve one set of problems in order to free oneself to move to another set. Perpetual problem solving can be taken as a model for teaching. The teacher, after having solved a classroom problem or, at any rate, after having evaluated his attempts to solve it, will still be alert and will identify new problems. The diagram below depicts the cyclical nature of the problem-solving sequence.

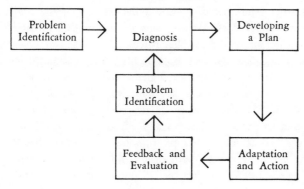

## A Case Study

The following case study will illustrate the problem-solving sequence step by step.

11

### Phase 1: Identifying the Classroom Problems

The problems that Mrs. Monroe was having with her classroom were fully described in Chapter One. She was concerned about the poor performance of her students, their lack of confidence, and their inability to work together or help each other in academic tasks. The peer relations seemed to lower students' self-esteem and initiative for academic tasks.

### Phase 2: Diagnosing the Classroom Problems

She decided to augment her initial understanding with a sociometric instrument, since it is a most appropriate device for assessing how members of a group feel about one another. The students were asked to indicate the four classmates they liked the most, and the four they tended to look up to and follow. Mrs. Monroe asked additional questions to learn how they felt about themselves, their teacher, their performance in school, and their feelings about coming to school.

From the students' responses, Mrs. Monroe discovered that several well-liked and influential students had definite antilearning and antischool attitudes. Students who were selected as most influential and highly liked were also selected as being most uncooperative with the teacher. The classroom leaders therefore were working against her. Mrs. Monroe also learned that most of the students felt it was bad to participate in class activities or to ask the teacher for help. Most of the students who responded positively to her attempts to influence and teach were ignored or rejected by their peers. The classroom peer-group social structure and standards were revealed in some detail, and Mrs. Monroe could now begin to make specific plans for improving them.

To further refine her diagnostic understanding of the students' attitudes toward school, Mrs. Monroe considered how they might have been formed by community and familial forces.

It was her conclusion that most of her students came to school with antiadult and antischool attitudes. Parents and neighborhood peers generally did not see the school as a productive, helpful, or pleasant place. In addition, the neighborhood gangs and youth groups fostered activities in opposition to public authorities and adults in general. Thus some of her students had achieved their prestige and maintained their leadership by defying authority figures, both inside and outside the classroom. The other students clustered around their "courageous leaders" and followed their example. In this way antiteacher standards were fairly well established and continually reinforced.

### Phase 3: Developing a Plan

In order to work out a solution to this difficult problem, Mrs. Monroe decided to deal with some of the cultural barriers to student-teacher collaboration. She planned a student steering committee that would use the established peer leaders to develop more positive classroom standards. Mrs. Monroe felt that coercive teacher enforcement of classroom discipline would produce only a surface conformity, which would enable the negatively oriented leaders to persist in their successful attempts to undermine her efforts. A steering committee that would discuss classroom behavior and publicly evaluate classroom operations had the principal advantage of placing the classroom leaders in a responsible position of working in cooperation with the teacher instead of against her. Furthermore, public evaluation of daily progress would enable the entire class to reflect upon whether their standards and behavior were appropriate and effective ways of getting along in school. Mrs. Monroe decided also to let the class set up its own rules for classroom conduct with her advice and consent.

## Phase 4:  Adaptation and Action

In putting her ideas into practice, Mrs. Monroe took the following steps:

1. She appointed an initial steering committee of five highly popular and influential boys and girls. She felt that once the peer-group leaders accepted their responsibility and her counsel, it would be easier to work with the rest of the class. In other words, with the highly influential students on her side, it would be easier to win over the rest.

2. A tentative set of rules for classroom behavior and procedures was developed by the committee and discussed by the entire class. In this way the members of the class normally dependent on the leaders might come to share responsibility for regulating classroom behavior. The leaders, in turn, would be reinforced in their new roles by class recognition of them.

3. Once a week at lunchtime Mrs. Monroe held leadership training sessions for members of the committee. In particular, she gave these students many suggestions about how to lead discussions and facilitate group decision making.

4. One member of the steering committee served as a classroom observer each day. Mrs. Monroe rotated the observer among the members for two reasons. In the first place, such a rotation gave the steering committee an opportunity to receive objective information about their efforts from several sources. Secondly, it provided an opportunity for Mrs. Monroe to train individual students in skills of listening to, and watching for, problems in the classroom.

5. Each Friday afternoon the steering committee led a session reviewing the week's work and permitting a revision of the rules. At these weekly discussions the entire class publicly evaluated the advantages and disadvantages of the steering committee's suggestions. Such a program of public establishment and evaluation of standards and rules helped make

13

the management of classroom life a legitimate and important topic of concern and attention for all students.

6. A new steering committee was appointed by the old committee every three weeks in an attempt to diffuse responsibility for classroom management among the students of the class.

7. All the students in the class served on the steering committee before any of the original members served again, in order to prevent the formation of a permanent clique and in order to give all the students an opportunity to learn and practice leadership skills. By this procedure Mrs. Monroe felt that the sociometric leaders could learn skills in group membership and cooperation that were at least as important as leadership skills.

### Phase 5: Feedback and Evaluation

Mrs. Monroe got feedback from the entire class in the weekly discussions that she had built into the action phase.

In making her own evaluation at the end of the year, she said that seventeen of her twenty-one students felt the steering committee idea had been a significant help. Some of the students who tended to be overly strict in the formulation and application of rules felt that they had received some help in becoming more flexible and understanding. Mrs. Monroe also reported some very significant gains in the level of student responsibility for classroom management. Since they had been entrusted with setting standards for classroom behavior, the students began to obey their own rules and to pay more attention to what was being taught. There was also a slight drop in the influence of the antischool, antiteacher students, since many other students now shared responsibility for classroom leadership. Mrs. Monroe felt that there was considerably less antagonism and resistance to her in particular and to school activities in general. Students seemed to be more interested in what was going on in class; they paid more attention, and asked for help when they needed it. In essence, Mrs. Monroe felt that the students were more willing to accept and respond positively to her teaching efforts.

# CHAPTER THREE

# Identifying Classroom Problems

In this first phase of the problem-solving process, the teacher tries to identify the major problems or concerns in the classroom. A problem exists when there is a discrepancy between the actual and the desired state of affairs. In order to identify problems in his classroom, a teacher must have a clear notion of his goals for the students and be sensitive to the processes of the classroom. Clear goals point the teacher to where he desires to lead his class. Sensitivity to classroom processes gives him information about discrepancies between the current state of affairs and the desired state.

In some cases the state of affairs in the classroom is obviously unsatisfactory or intolerable, as when one or several students are constantly inattentive, withdrawn, or disruptive. In others it may be a tolerable situation that could be improved, as when students are only minimally attentive and responsive. Both these kinds of problems are potentially resolvable. There is another type of problem that is perennial: how to help students reach their fullest potential for learning and growth. The objective is never achieved, but much energy can be expended and much satisfaction gained in its pursuit. All classrooms present problems that require attention; the type and magnitude of the problem vary considerably from class to class.

Most classroom problems involve both the academic performance and the personal development of the students. Sometimes they are recognized primarily through the students' failures to make academic progress, as seen by poor performance on examinations. Problems may be more subtly evident in a low level of student involvement or interest in academic assignments. A teacher may observe that some students are not attending carefully to the subject matter being presented, that they are bored and lackadaisical, or that they pass notes and joke during class discussions. Low involvement in learning also may be revealed by the students' inability to take initiative or responsibility for their own growth, as when they find it very difficult to work on their own or are dependent solely on the teacher for intellectual stimulation and growth.

Classroom problems may, on the other hand, be brought to the teacher's attention by the ways in which students relate to peers in the classroom, the ways they relate to adults, and the ways in which they conduct themselves in general. Students who exhibit little self-discipline and initiative in nonacademic aspects of classroom life are clearly not fully effective as students. Moreover, students who are rejected by their peers and those who are not able to get along well with others may also cause concern for the teacher not only because they are lonely, but also because they may engage in bizarre and disruptive behavior in attempts to relate more effectively. Many students who are isolated or rejected by their peers also experience difficulty achieving in academic areas. Another example of students who are minimizing their personal growth in the class are those who are timid and seldom or never ask questions. Other students may act aggressive and express themselves by asking facetious questions or bullying others.

Intuition and the experience of frustration will indicate that there is a problem, but the teacher should be prepared to use scientific knowledge of the dynamics of classroom interaction to interpret it. It is not enough for him to roughly identify the problem as academic or behavioral, since academic and behavioral difficulties are often two aspects of the same problem.

It is helpful for the teacher to make some distinctions between classroom problems that are relevant to individual students, those that are shared by groups of students, and those that are primarily related to his own personality and teaching style.* After the teacher has identified the area into which the problem falls, he is ready to proceed with a diagnosis of the situation; but without this general identification of the problem, attempts to collect diagnostic data and plan for action will be indiscriminate and haphazard.

## Individual Student Behavior

Some examples of individual student problems are low involvement in learning, little initiative or responsibility in learning tasks, inadequate academic performance, and disruptive social behavior. Some of these problems may be related to a poor image of self or to negative attitudes that the student brings with him into the classroom. It is possible to diagnose such problems as individual personality concerns and treat them by personal counseling and individual attention. These are legitimate

---

*For a more extensive and detailed discussion of these classroom characteristics and others, the reader should turn to *Understanding Classroom Social Relations and Learning*. The conceptual frameworks and research findings presented there should further help the teacher to refine his understanding of classroom difficulties.

approaches, but they are not within the scope of this booklet. The problem-solving process presented here will treat individual problems in the context of classroom social forces.

The merit of this situational approach lies in the fact that the student is a member of a group, and therefore his attitudes and behavior do not stand alone. They may be exacerbated by the relations he has with others in the classroom and, in turn, may worsen the classroom learning climate. Individual difficulties may easily be reinforced by the group: as the student relates negatively to others, they relate negatively to him, confirming him in his disruptive, withdrawn, or irresponsible behavior.

As students interact and students and teachers relate, they will give indications as to how they feel about one another. These signs of feeling influence to some degree how a student views himself, his abilities, his likability, and his general worth. These feelings or evaluations of himself make up a student's self-esteem, which is clearly related to his utilization of academic potential and his future occupational and educational aspirations.

In addition to difficulties in academic performance, youngsters with poor self-images tend to dislike and be disliked by other students and to perpetuate uncomfortable social relations. Children involved in these situations often are unable to concentrate on their academic subject matter. Classroom disturbances will tend to proliferate where children have poor self-images. Sometimes teachers unwittingly exacerbate such problems and, by scolding or punishing, perpetuate negative self-images and uncontrolled behavior.

When the teacher is thinking about problems of self-esteem, he should ask questions such as these: Are there some students who tend to be left out of most classroom activities? Are there some who are always chosen first, and others who are always last? Are there some students who appear bothered, hostile, or withdrawn? He should also examine his own behavior and attitudes: How do I distribute rewards and punishments in the classroom? Are there certain children to whom I give primarily negative criticism and rebuke, and others who receive a large portion of the praise? Do I give negative criticism in ways that help rather than hinder student growth?

## The Classroom Peer Group

As the teacher recognizes to what extent individual student attitudes and behavior are conditioned by and influence other students, he will see that many classroom problems can only be understood by analyzing classroom peer relations. These problems must be dealt with as problems of groups of students or of the classroom peer group as a whole. The

17

following analysis of the classroom peer group, broken into two parts, is a behavioral-science approach to understanding classroom group behavior.

## Peer Relations

The teacher might ask: What kinds of peer relations distinguish this class? Are there generally friendly and cooperative relationships between the students, or is there a lot of aggression and hostility? Are there many students who seem to be popular, or just a few well-liked youngsters and several others who are disliked and excluded from activities? How do the students work together on cooperative tasks? Do just a few students dominate classroom discussions or group activities? Are there some groups of students who persistently ignore or reject others? Is there an "in" group or clique that makes the other students uncomfortable in class?

Students interacting in the classroom develop some consistent ways of behaving and relating to one another. Some of them assume leadership, others follow; some lead in class, others lead on the playground. In some classrooms boys and girls play together; in other classrooms they stay far apart. Students develop and maintain regular and stable patterns of informal classroom relations which are referred to as the group structure.

Classroom peer-group structures show striking differences in the ways friendship and influence relations are distributed. Some class groups show a hierarchical pattern with high consensus on who is at the top and bottom of the peer status structure, and others show a more diffuse structure with a larger number of students receiving a share of the positive affective and status evaluations. Higher classroom morale and maximum student utilization of ability are associated with the diffusion of friendship and influence choices throughout the group.

These informal relations among peers, from which group structure emerges, have important effects on the way the students conceive of and carry out the more formal academic demands of the classroom. This is especially the case when peer likability patterns become intensely intimate and affective. Indeed, the more importance peer relations have for the individual student, the more they affect his definition and evaluation of self, and the more psychologically threatening or supportive they can become. The more threatening or supportive these relations become, the more probability they have of affecting an individual student's adjustments to academic tasks.

Because the peer group structure has a demonstrably important effect on the way group members expend their intellectual and emotional energies, it is important for the teacher to know something about it. A classroom group structure is observable easily from the results of sociometric questions or from carefully planned observations. Information on the group structure usually tells which students are leaders, followers, isolates, or rejectees; it also includes data on group pressures that form when some students become more popular than others and are able to exert great influence. In addition to the social power or influence that one individual may exert on another, students collectively can exert social pressure on other students. These pressures can either encourage or inhibit an individual's comfort and his use of his unique talents.

The teacher should also know that his influence on peer acceptance patterns in the classroom can be quite basic. In one demonstration teachers were instructed to attend to and reward only the students in odd-numbered seats and to ignore or punish the other youngsters. Several weeks later the students were given some questions on whom they would like to sit near and work with. Results showed that the students who were rewarded by the teachers were chosen more often than the others; the teachers had substantially formed the group structures of their classes. Similarly, a teacher can increase the spread of friendship in the class by showing acceptance of those youngsters who are being neglected or rejected by their peers.

## Classroom Group Norms

As the classroom group forms into a relatively stable structure, shared attitudes and standardized ways of behaving become accepted and enforced. These overtly or covertly agreed-upon ways of thinking and behaving are termed norms or standards. The norms and structural arrangements of the classroom group influence individual attitudes, interests, and motivations.

Such norms as a belief that it is good to take part as much as possible in classroom work, that asking the teacher for guidance is a good thing to do, and that schoolwork is fun may be important for the classroom group. Peer norms regarding the teacher, academic work, and individual differences are important influences on the classroom learning climate.

Often classroom standards are established that keep students from asking for help in academic matters. The result may be that they are afraid to utilize the resources available in the classroom. Some of these resources may be material, such as textbooks or a small library; others may be social, such as peers or teachers. If the teacher has set up a library and most of the students use it, he may decide that lack of utilization of resources is an individual problem for a few students. However, failure of a large group of students to use this library may be seen as a problem of the classroom group, probably of group norms.

Every classroom group has its own norms for appropriate behavior, its own "rules of the game." When a deviant student disobeys these norms he may be sanctioned by peer disapproval or rejection. Sometimes the

19

norms support the teacher's efforts and sometimes they do not. In some cases the norms may be unclear, and students have a hard time understanding what is appropriate and proper behavior at any one time. A teacher who sees a lot of inappropriate behavior among a large number of students may well inquire into whether the standards of this class have been clearly and publicly set; and whether these rules have been set with or without the consent of many of the students.

Norms are enforced by social pressures that the majority of the peers, or a minority of strong leaders, exert on the norm breakers. The low-peer-status pupil often is one who has broken some set of classroom norms and is thereby ostracized and rejected by his peers. In addition to the obviousness of rejection, much more subtle components of group conformity take place in classroom peer groups, so that sometimes students behave in accordance with norms although oblivious of the pressures on them. Once developed, class standards may so influence students' interaction patterns that the teacher himself may be frustrated or inhibited from teaching in his preferred manner.

Positive peer relations and supportive norms together make up a classroom atmosphere characterized by feelings of freedom and mutual respect that stimulate the development of the student's intellectual resources and social skills. Interpersonal relations in the classroom that demonstrate to youngsters that their abilities are respected and their participation and involvement are desired create group atmospheres conducive to learning. Children can be forced to go to school, but cannot be forced to learn; it is a supportive group atmosphere that best induces and rewards a student's motivation to come to school and to try actively to learn.

## Teacher-Student Relations

Another major cluster of problems, in addition to those of individuals and of peer-group relations are found in the relations between teacher and students. The teacher may see examples of these problems when his attempts at influence and instruction meet with passivity, inattention, or rejection. Of course, teacher ineffectiveness may be an individual student problem or a problem in classroom norms and standards, but it also may be an instance of a lack of clear communication between students and the teacher. Other examples of problems between teachers and students are teacher dominance of the students, and a teaching style that seriously frightens or threatens them or one that is overly permissive. The teacher who plays favorites or distributes rewards and praise arbitrarily and unevenly may alienate some students. Those who feel they are being neglected or treated unfairly, or who fear their teacher, may often be paralyzed in their attempts to work well academically or express themselves in the class. Such paralysis and inhibition is clearly detrimental to emotional and intellectual growth. In cases where the students are consistently inattentive, unhappy, rejecting, or resistant to the teacher or the learning material, the teacher does well to inquire into his own relationship with these students and its potential for creating inhibitory and negative learning situations.

For instance, if a student turns and looks in another direction when the teacher talks to him, the teacher has received information that the student was not listening or did not like what the teacher said or did. In most cases the reception of information from others helps one to adjust his behavior accordingly, but it is difficult for the teacher who has been rejected to respond positively and supportively to the resisting student. Often, then, the teacher encounters students who are not receiving enough constructive comments and rewards and thus cannot adjust their behavior to make themselves more effective classroom participants.

Teachers and students attempt to satisfy their respective desires by working out a comfortable and stable relationship with each other; both attempt to modify or adapt their behaviors to make them more mutually acceptable. For instance, a student may not wish to stand in line to go outdoors but accedes to the teacher's request. On the other hand, a teacher may not want the children involved in boisterous play, but will allow them to let off steam on the playground so long as they walk out quietly from the classroom. Here both the student and the teacher have modified what they really want to do in a specific situation so that their behaviors are generally acceptable to each other. All people engage in such mutual adaptations when they undertake to develop and maintain an interpersonal relationship. What creative teachers seek is a pattern of mutual adaptation that promotes the most fruitful classroom atmosphere for learning.

Relations between teachers and students can be conveniently conceptualized as a stable and circular interpersonal process. The circular process is a relationship cycle between any two persons that is maintained by unconscious mutual reinforcements. There are many possibilities; one kind would be a positive cycle. When the student enters the classroom with a positive evaluation of his own competence and likability, often he perceives that the teacher positively evaluates him; and he, in turn, likes the teacher. The student's behaviors toward the teacher show a balance of seeking and offering, and of relatively open acceptance of the teacher's approaches. The teacher interprets this behavior as one of friendliness and acceptance, and he reacts accordingly in a positive and supportive way. A continuing cycle of positive evaluation emerges between the two along with a sense of shared rewards and enhancement.

Examples of negative cycles also occur often in the classrooms. In one, the student comes to the class with positive feelings of his own resources but perceives himself as negatively evaluated by the teacher, whom he also tends to dislike. This often results in a pattern of hostility from the student and active resistance and rejection by the teacher. The teacher perceives the student's behaviors as unfriendly and resistant to change, while from the student's point of view, the teacher continuously acts in a threatening and hostile manner, and these teacher behaviors confirm the student's distrust. Such a pattern establishes a mutual cycle of distrust and nonproductive classroom activity.

Another type of negative cycle occurs when the student has a personal conception of inadequacy and perceives the teacher as much more adequate and possessing envied skills. The student's behaviors toward the teacher are dependent and demanding, and the teacher, with a positive self-conception, perceives these student behaviors as too demanding and distracting and often as involving latent hostility. The teacher reacts with a combination of unfriendly, dominating, avoiding, and resisting behaviors. The student perceives these as rejection, his feelings of inadequacy are deepened, and a stable cycle of unfriendly rejection and avoidance is established and maintained.

The concepts useful for understanding the classroom discussed in this chapter are highly interrelated and operate together in creating a climate for social and academic learning. Individuals come into class with characteristics that influence the way students and teacher relate to one another. The social structure of the peer group and the group norms both affect the amount and direction of influence attempts and feedback in the classroom. Peer relations and information gained from feedback by teacher or other students serve to give the individual student a reflection of his worth and esteem, through the eyes of others. All these factors influence and are influenced by the kinds of informal working relations and unconscious circular processes that define the more formal relations between individual student and teacher, between the classroom group and the teacher, and among the students themselves.

# CHAPTER FOUR

# Diagnosing Classroom Problems

In this phase of solving classroom problems the teacher diagnoses the dynamics of student attitudes and behavior. Although the sensitive teacher is always attending to the nuances of student behavior and classroom interaction, careful and systematic diagnosis is valuable for the planning of constructive classroom change. Simple diagnostic tools and observational techniques can be used to get an accurate picture of students' feelings, attitudes, and classroom social relations. Thus the teacher's observations of student behavior and his preliminary analyses of them according to behavioral science theories are supplemented with objective and detailed knowledge of what exactly is happening in his classroom.

The teacher cannot plan change in his classroom unless he knows exactly what is going on there. All too often, the interpretations that a teacher will make of the behavior in his classroom will be totally inaccurate. If he proceeds with changes on the basis of his inaccurate interpretations, he may very well do more harm than good. Often, for example, a teacher may think that the larger, more boisterous, more disruptive boys in his class are the peer leaders, when the administration of a sociometric instrument might show that the majority of their classmates actively dislike them. Just as often, the reverse may be the case: the teacher may think that the bright and cooperative students have greater influence with their classmates than they actually do. A teacher wanting to improve the classroom learning climate by forming small work groups may, on the basis of his inaccurate interpretations, choose leaders for these groups who do not have the social skills to keep the members of the group productive. A teacher who erroneously thinks that the more boisterous students are class leaders may work to diminish their influence, when in fact these students may have very little influence to begin with. Another example of erroneous interpretation of student behavior might be the teacher who thinks that the boredom and inattention displayed by his students is caused by the negative attitudes about school they get at home, when in fact appropriate diagnostic instruments may reveal that his teaching style is boring, dominating, and generally insensitive to the feelings and needs of his students.

A companion booklet in this series, *Diagnosing Classroom Learning Environments,* details twenty-three different instruments that have proved useful in diagnosing classroom atmospheres and describes how the data obtained by them can be recorded, interpreted, and used. By a systematic use of these instruments, the complex behavior patterns of a classroom can be analyzed from a variety of perspectives. Thus, by using various tools, a teacher can examine a single set of phenomena, such as lack of cooperation and support among students, in terms of peer attitudes, students' self-esteem, the teacher's style, students' conceptions of their own role in the classroom, parental expectations of student performance, and other factors.

One of the aims of diagnosis is to integrate the problems noticed in the problem-identification phase, so that they can be dealt with as a unit rather than piecemeal. The teacher, for example, who sees that some of his students are disruptive of orderly classroom procedures, that others are bored and inattentive, that some do their work conscientiously but passively and uncreatively, that others are overly dependent on him, that some get so enthusiastic about the subject matter that they dominate all classroom discussions, is advised in the diagnostic stage to look for common factors that may be influencing all these behaviors. Otherwise, in developing plans later for improving the classroom, he may work on these problems one by one, expending much time and effort with little result. These behaviors should be viewed as symptoms, and just as a physician tries to treat the causes underlying symptoms, so should the teacher. In the diagnostic stage the teacher seeks exact knowledge of the symptoms of the poor classroom learning environment so that he can find the underlying problems that integrate these symptoms.

In general, there are two ways in which a teacher can proceed with his diagnosis: through the use of questionnaires and through classroom observational techniques. Often these two methods are best used to complement one another. Moreover, questions can be either forced- or multiple-choice or open-ended. Some questionnaires make use of both types; others limit themselves to one. *Diagnosing Classroom Learning Environments* discusses the limitations and advantages of these different types of questions and shows how each can best be used.

Questionnaires often can be utilized to get information concerning students' feelings about themselves. In addition, assessments of this nature for all students in the classroom may give the teacher a gross index of the way the students perceive themselves as being evaluated by him. There is often a discrepancy between what the teacher judges students to be feeling and the way they actually do feel. Since students act according to their own views of themselves, it is important to assess and understand their self-perceptions. There are several types of inventories for assessing self-feelings, including the attitude survey, the sentence-completion test, and the so-called pie technique.

An example of an attitude survey item regarding work habits:

How hard would you say that you are working on school work? (Circle one)
A. Very hard
B. Pretty hard
C. Not very hard
D. Not hard at all

A sentence-completion item of the same general character:

When I am doing schoolwork, I feel_____.

Or, in measuring different aspects of feelings about self:

I like myself sometimes because_____.
When I think about other boys and girls and then think about myself, I feel
_____.

The pie technique has been used as follows:

The pluses stand for working hard, the minuses for not working hard. Place a check under the circle that stands for how hard you usually work.

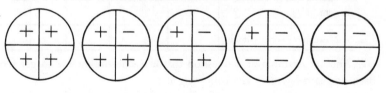

Student self-esteem, ranging from very positive to very negative, is expressed in these three sample responses drawn from a sentence-completion test:

When I look in a mirror, *I feel that I look good.*
When I look at other boys and girls and then look at myself, *I feel on the same level as they.*
Sometimes I think I am *a bad and naughty boy.*

Sociometric questions are especially designed to give the teacher some indication of the social relations among students in the class. He may ask students to tell which peers they like best, like to work with, like to play with, think are smartest, think like them, and like least. In this manner the teacher can see which children are friendly with each other and which are likely to make compatible work partners. With younger students all six of these dimensions of attraction are likely to show similar results; as the students grow older they tend to discriminate and make different choices for "liking," "working," "playing." In addition to getting information about pairings, the teacher can sum and rank individual choices to find out who the peer leaders are, whether there are cliques, and what the general interaction patterns are like. By summing and analyzing the responses for the entire class on these types of questions, the teacher can get some idea of the common attitudes of members of the class. Those common attitudes about school, teacher, or peers are the groundwork for the establishment of norms and enforcement of behavioral standards.

The teacher can analyze the students' feelings about his methods by asking them to suggest changes in the way he behaves. The format for the question might be as follows:

Pretend that you could have your teacher change in some way. Please mark the way you would like to have your teacher act by checking the box that best tells how you would like him to be.

|  | Much more | A little more | The same | Less | Much less |
|---|---|---|---|---|---|
| 1. Help with work |  |  |  |  |  |
| 2. Yell at us |  |  |  |  |  |
| 3. Make sure work is done |  |  |  |  |  |

Another example of a question that a teacher might use to get feedback on his behavior is the following item:

Here is a list of some things that describe life in the classroom. Circle the number of the statement that best tells how this class is for you.

Life in this class with your regular teacher has
1. all good things
2. mostly good things
3. more good things than bad
4. about as many good things as bad
5. more bad things than good
6. mostly bad things

Open-ended questions that indirectly measure students' reactions to the teacher's methods can also be used. One questionnaire, entitled "Clues of a Classroom Day," asks the following questions:

What are some clues of a good day in our class?
What are some clues of a bad day in our class?
What are some things that should happen a lot more than they do to make it a better class?

Another way of assessing student feelings about the teacher is to ask them to complete the following incomplete sentences: What I like most about my teacher is _____; What I like least about my teacher is _____.

The information that the teacher gets with tools such as these may enable him to work on his relations with specific pupils or on his general approach to all pupils, or to feel encouraged that his pupils think things are going well.

The teacher can use a variety of observational techniques for diagnosing the social relations in the classroom. He might assess interpersonal relations by constructing graphs of communication in the classroom or the playground. For instance, he can graph the flow of conversations during free-play time, trace the character and sequence of physical activity during recreation, or note which pupils talk to one another in a congenial or noncongenial fashion. In addition, of course, he can supplement these observations with a sociometric test or an attitudinal questionnaire to check his own perceptions.

Highly detailed observational techniques have been developed to analyze the nature of teacher-student interactions. Chapter Five of *Diagnosing Classroom Learning Environments* discusses two such methods. The interested teacher is advised to refer to that chapter. Here it can be mentioned that the procedure developed by Flanders is especially appropriate to the diagnosis of these interaction patterns. It distinguishes three very general types of classroom interaction: (1) indirect teacher influence including accepting feelings, praising, accepting ideas, and asking questions, (2) direct teacher influences including lecturing, giving directions, and criticizing behavior, and (3) student talk including initiated remarks and responses.

The teacher will find it difficult to use Flanders' scheme on his own. Better use could be made of this technique by finding an outside observer, preferably a colleague, who could come into the classroom and objectively describe the patterns of interaction by using these categories. In any case, before the teacher tries out the categories he should consult *Diagnosing Classroom Learning Environments* for a fuller discussion of the method and references for Flanders' publications.

The use of diagnostic tools should allow the student to feel secure in expressing negative feelings about the classroom. Also, in a classroom where prevailing peer attitudes make it difficult for any child to overtly display enthusiasm about the learning process, these tools may show the teacher that some of his students have positive attitudes and feelings about school that they ordinarily conceal from their classmates. Indeed, one of the important functions of diagnostic tools is to provide teacher and students with a formal, objective, and confidential means of receiving personal reactions about their behavior. Questionnaires can be filled out anonymously, but since valuable information about individual and sub-group attitudes is lost this way, the teacher is often best advised to convince the students that the information received will be used only to benefit them and that no one will be punished or criticized for his responses.

The teacher furthermore should exercise some restraint in the collection of diagnostic data; he should seek only information that can be used to enhance the students' academic and personal development. In addition, he would be wise to employ diagnostic tools extensively only with the approval and confidence of his principal and be prepared to explain his objectives and methods to his colleagues or to interested parents.

Most diagnostic instruments can and should be used during two phases of the problem-solving sequence. First of all, they are to be used in the diagnostic phase. Secondly, after the teacher has planned and carried out a change in classroom practices, diagnostic instruments should be used to obtain feedback on the immediate effects of the new practice and to evaluate the long-term effects on the learning environment of the classroom. These latter uses of the instruments will be discussed at greater length in Chapter Nine.

# CHAPTER FIVE

# *Cultural Influences on Classroom Problem Solving*

There are substantial data to suggest that a myriad of community and cultural influences affect the values, self-esteem, and work of the student in the classroom. Students come to school having problems they encountered with parents, neighborhood peers, teachers, principals, or other members of the youth socialization community. Classroom relations may make some of these problems easier or more difficult to handle, but in some cases a full mobilization of classroom resources may not help students at all. Perhaps only major changes in the home and neighborhood can help certain students deal with their concerns. For example, students whose families and neighborhoods are in conflict with one another cannot be expected to get along with one another in the classroom. Youngsters who come from broken or unstable homes may be irrevocably scarred.

The economy creates and maintains financial stratifications, and the country is additionally divided at every economic level by racial and ethnic distinctions. Students mirror these divisions as well as the influences of their familial and neighborhood customs and attitudes. The sum of these organized social influences make up the youngsters' culture, which is reflected in different personal and interpersonal styles of language, cognitive development, levels of aspiration and achievement, and attitudes. Though the teacher cannot influence these extraschool factors directly, he should consider them while developing a plan for improving the classroom atmosphere in order that he can focus on problems that are most amenable to treatment in the classroom.

## Social Class Differences

Social class is defined in various ways by sociologists, and each of these definitions can be helpful in understanding classroom behavior. Because of differences in material and educational resources, people differ in status or prestige, in social power, and in interests and concerns. People who are in the middle or upper classes make more money and typically have higher educational levels than those in the lower classes. They are also accorded more prestige in the community and thus exert influence upon the ways in which people interact and upon the decisions made in face-to-face groups. In addition, people in the same social class tend to have similar interests, attitudes, values, and goals. Very often, class identifications are strengthened by the housing and working patterns of the community. It is not uncommon to find an upper-middle-class section of town in which business leaders, doctors, lawyers, and other high-status families live; a lower-middle-class part of town where lower white-collar workers, salesmen, and skilled laborers live; and a lower-class part of town where the unskilled and unemployed live. People of the same social class tend to relate to one another often, to experience a similar environment, to arrive at similar perspectives on life, to rear their children in similar ways, and to approach education with relatively common outlooks and expectations.

Some behaviors of youngsters in school can be seen as a function of their understanding of social class differences. There are youngsters, for example, who think that prestige and power must be gained through popularity; these youngsters may put so much energy into extracurricular activities that they fall behind in their studies. There are also students who see academic competence as a path to peer respect and popularity. Some students are so closely identified with their neighborhood and family values and habits that they fear to interact in extracurricular groups that expose them to students of different backgrounds. Since the values of middle-class families are usually emphasized in American schools, lower-class youngsters may feel that school achievement calls upon them to betray their backgrounds. This attitude is reflected in the notion that academic enthusiasm is for sissies. A student trained in the more verbal forms of expression used in middle-class families may himself be intimidated and made to feel a sissy when surrounded in the classroom by his more physically active lower-class peers. He may deliberately throttle some of his interests and abilities so as not to appear too different from them. Most teachers are highly verbal in their teaching, thereby placing a premium upon the communication styles most comfortable to middle-class youngsters. Lower-class youngsters are more accustomed to active, motoric styles of expression, and become more involved and perform better when there is some mixture of these teaching approaches. A teacher who recognizes this possibility can plan to teach in a way that effectively communicates to his various students and involves all of them in learning activities. In some communities, and consequently in some classrooms, relations between students of different social class backgrounds may be fraught with misunderstanding, distrust, and prejudice. Instead of seeing legitimate differences between styles of living and learning, students frequently make negative evaluations of these differences and even further frustrate collaborative learning. In order to deal with these varied interclass and interpersonal issues, the teacher will need to use some of the information presented in this chapter.*

In order to secure information about students' backgrounds, the teacher can search school records or ask students about parental employment and occupational roles. Another good indicator of social class, and one that is especially useful within similar occupational or income levels, is parental education.

## Racial Differences

Racial difference is another important cultural factor that teachers should keep in mind. There are few reliable data available to behavioral scientists that indicate that there are basic innate differences of intelligence, attitudes, or other personality characteristics between the races. These differences exist in our society because of the different ways in which Negroes and Caucasians have been socialized and the lack of economic and social opportunities available to the Negro. Because of the complex factors involved in the economic and political history of this country, most American Negroes are members of the lower class. Many of the characteristics that the Negro child manifests are better understood as a consequence of class membership than of race.

There are, however, other problems that arise not so much because of class differences, although these are very important, as because of caste differences. For years whites and Negroes have been viewed by many citizens as qualitatively different, as formed from different stock with basically different genetic, psychological, and spiritual characteristics. Thus many of the principles that separate castes in India are applied to racial differences in our society. So long as black and white are seen as basically different, the American Negro will suffer from some of the effects of belonging to an "inferior caste."

---

*A companion booklet in this series, *Role-Playing Methods in the Classroom,* describes ways in which role playing can be used to help youngsters from different backgrounds better understand, interact with, and learn from each other.

Naturally, special stresses are put on the Negro child in our society. The most basic stems from the discrepancy between the theories of democratic values and equality, and the practice of enforced or de facto segregation. A popular American myth pronounces that every American man regardless of his social background has an equal opportunity to succeed and that the most important ingredient of success is hard work. Because this myth is voiced in many books and through the mass media, while simultaneously many occupations, public places, and even the voting franchise in some states are denied to the Negro, many Negroes feel intense frustrations that are often expressed in the classroom.

As a result of personal, familial, and cultural conflicts, the Negro youngster can easily overgeneralize about white people. His impression may be that all whites are somehow conspiring against him. The teacher who is white, and an authority, is often seen as being a representative of those conspiring against him. With little trust in the teacher, and with suppressed negative feelings toward him, the Negro child is often unable to cooperate and learn academic subject matter very easily. Often the teacher interprets such performance as an example of antisocial attitudes and poor intellectual abilities, and a negative circular process between teacher and student similar to that discussed in Chapter Three can develop.

## The Link Between Family Life and School Performance

Two general explanations for the relation between low social status and low school adjustment are usually offered. The first emphasizes the material environment in the home. It is argued that a varied environment and a variety of stimuli during early development, conditions more likely to be found in middle-class than in lower-class homes, are more conducive to higher utilization of a child's intellectual potential than impoverished and monotonous environments.

A second, more social-psychological explanation, and the one that will be stressed in the following discussion, emphasizes the lack of orientation of lower-class parents to education and the discontinuity between the values and requirements of the lower-class family and the demands and expectations of the school. Most middle-class children are taught the importance of intellectual skills through the conversations and urgings of their parents. Success in reading, writing, and arithmetic take on great significance, for the middle-class child learns that these modes of expression are of value in themselves. Youngsters growing up in lower-class subcultures, in contrast, often learn anti-intellectual attitudes. Although education is typically seen as a valuable commodity by the lower-class as well as the middle-class parent, the emphasis in the lower class is mostly pragmatic; the parent is primarily interested in the child's becoming respectable and getting an adequate job as a consequence of school experiences. Learning for its own sake and for intellectual development is emphasized less in the lower-class than in the middle-class home.

When the values of the family and the school are contradictory, the children have little incentive for school advancement. When the values of home and school are harmonious, however, achievement in school leads to recognition and praise at home. Such supportive experiences in the home, especially when they are perceived as such by the child, increase academic motivation and build positive attitudes toward school. Both of these student attitudes, in turn, lead to fuller utilization of intellectual potential.

Thus a circular process develops, with the parents' attitudes toward school influencing their child's achievement efforts, and the child's achievements in turn influencing parental attitudes. Sometimes, for instance, a child's school success reflects credit on the parents, making them feel more positive toward school, and these feelings may be reflected in the child's perception of his parents' attitudes, which will reinforce his own positive attitudes. On the other hand, a child's lack of immediate success in school could result in the parents' feelings becoming increasingly more negative toward school, and also toward the child as a student. This is especially true of parents who are not academically oriented in the first place or whose own school experiences were unpleasant. In any case, a stable relationship develops between parents and child with the parents' attitudes and conceptions about school reinforcing the child's. Since parents' attitudes are so crucial to school adjustment, the teacher should know something about them. Incomplete sentences and stories are means of obtaining a student's perceptions of and feelings about his parents' attitudes. A variety of diagnostic tools and methods to explore these attitudes is presented in Chapter Seven of *Diagnosing Classroom Learning Environments.*

## Teacher Cultural Background

Nearly all teachers come from middle-class backgrounds. They live in moderately priced houses; their fathers often have had some college education, and they have some status and power in the community. In contrast to this pattern, well over half of the children in American classrooms come from working-class, lower-class, and deprived backgrounds. Consequently the interests, values, attitudes, and behavioral styles of many teachers and students differ, and very often conflicts develop because of these differences. There is not necessarily any conscious intent behind such conflicts; they simply arise because of basically different sociocultural experiences.

Teachers are also predominantly Caucasian or upwardly mobile Negroes, and consequently have some difficulty in empathizing with the problems and concerns of lower-status Negro students. In order for a teacher to be successful in teaching lower-status Negroes, he must be sensitive to their cultural experiences. He must gain trust, respect, and rapport, while attempting to teach the child language skills, arithmetic, history, and other subjects. The teacher must show the minority child that he is on his side, that he agrees that some whites are bigoted, and that together they will try to understand and overcome this situation. Such thoughts and feelings of the teacher are often necessary prerequisites to a successful lower-class Negro classroom.

## Psycho-social Characteristics of Middle- and Lower-Class Students

Given these commonly occurring differences among students and between students and teachers, it would be useful for the teacher to compare some of the basic social-psychological characteristics of children who grow up in a middle-class culture with those who grow up in the lower-class areas of the community. The following discussion will describe these characteristics dichotomously, contrasting a secure middle class where occupational prestige, education, and income are all high with a deprived lower class where these same social factors are all low. The contrast is rather extreme, and is used primarily for convenience of presentation; the teacher will realize that although there are many students who exhibit all the characteristics of the described middle class and many who are like the described lower class, there will be many students who have characteristics of both groups. This occurs, for example, when income is high and occupational prestige and education are low, or when education is high and occupational prestige and income are low.

### Language Skills

Because his familial and neighborhood experiences are in contrast to those of the lower-class child, the middle-class student generally has more skill in language. He has watched his parents reading, has played word games with them, and has already learned some dictionary skills. He has engaged in lengthy discussions in which he has been encouraged to initiate ideas and to listen to what others are saying. The middle-class child learns that he can show off and please his parents by having memorized something. The lower-class child, on the other hand, does not receive the same support for memorizing rhymes, jokes, prayers, and other sayings. The lower-class child has engaged in little if any extensive discussion at home. Often he is given commands with a minimum of verbal communication. The expressions that his parents use are often very short and at times they are not full sentences or complete ideas. The child has probably seldom seen his parents reading, and has gotten few rewards for showing verbal skills.

By the time they are around two years old, children from lower socio-economic groups already have inferior verbal skills in comparison with those of the middle class. It seems inevitable that even at the first-grade level, low-status children would not perform well on verbal aspects of the curriculum. It should be expected, then, that lower-class students, in contrast to middle-class students, would do poorer on intelligence tests which are heavily weighted with measures of verbal and conceptual skills. The child is asked to think abstractly using terminology that he may never have heard. He is asked to identify animals when he may never have been to a zoo. He is asked to identify symphonic instruments when he may not know what an orchestra is.

Some psychologists question whether the differences in average intelligence scores between high- and low-status students are valid. Since the experiences for the different social class groups vary widely, and since the styles of expression that the students will be familiar with are so different, the lower-class student is at a disadvantage on such tests. Most psychologists believe that the social class differences in intelligence may be a reflection of a bias in favor of verbally skilled higher-status groups and not an indication of basic ability differences.

Teachers should look with some skepticism on total intelligence test scores, and be advised that it is often more valuable to know something about the various scale scores. The teacher should certainly attend to language and nonlanguage skill differences when working with lower-class children. When a large discrepancy exists between language and quantitative parts of the test, with the quantitative items being much higher, the low language score may be due to verbal deprivations at home, biased test items, or both. Such children probably have considerably more potential than the tests indicate.

## Conceptual Development and Expressive Styles

Middle-class children tend to live in a conceptual and verbal world, while lower-class children have had much more experience expressing themselves physically and motorically. Lower-class children are more often physically punished by their parents, and their interpersonal relations usually involve expressions of bodily movement, gestures, and touch, both affectionate and aggressive. Thus they are much more physical in expressing themselves. Often middle-class teachers have problems in understanding that lower-class interpersonal relations, though seemingly very aggressive, do not have that meaning for the students much of the time.

The aggressiveness that occurs in the lower-class home teaches the    35 student that the body is a vehicle for interpersonal relations; consequently physical aggression among some lower-class groups is regarded as normal. Fighting is common in the student's family and neighborhood, and he learns to be aggressive when he is frustrated or needs to express himself. Since the middle-class teacher has learned that aggression and fighting are signs of an immature individual, he tends to treat the lower-class student as being only partially developed. Thus the teacher can easily rationalize his failure to teach the child the concepts that would help him develop verbally.

In one experimental study it was found that adolescent boys from the working class predominantly were motoric rather than verbal when playing games, painting pictures, or choosing hobbies and jobs. On the other hand, boys from the middle class were more verbal and abstract and less motoric in their reactions to these same activities. Familial child-rearing practices are significantly related to these different expressive styles. A verbal or conceptual orientation is typically associated with psychological discipline, symbolic reward, and maternal self-control. Some evidence indicates that middle-class parents usually discipline their children psychologically and reward them verbally or symbolically. A motoric orientation is more characteristically associated with lower-class patterns of corporal discipline, concrete reward, and the parents' loss of self-control.

When the teacher is trying to diagnose the attitudes and feelings of youngsters in the classroom, he should remember that the middle-class student, unless of low intelligence, can respond more easily to a paper-and-pencil diagnosis and to abstract questions than the lower-class student. The teachers of lower-class students might try to obtain attitudinal information by using more concrete diagnostic tools. For instance, feedback from students about how they felt during a class period could be obtained by asking those who felt good about the class hour to put a check beneath a smiling face, those who felt neutral to check an indifferent face, and those who felt negatively to check a frowning face (see Chapter Nine).

### Level of Aspiration
The middle-class child tends to have a high level of aspiration when he arrives at school. Very often the lower-class child starts with a high level of aspiration also, but as he experiences frustrations with the instructions and conversations of the teacher, he is unable to succeed easily. A lack of success leads to a reduction in the child's level of aspiration and expectations. As the level of aspiration goes down, the child's performance level goes down even further, because he believes that he cannot do well. This process is self-reinforcing and can go on and on.

Negro youngsters often have problems in maintaining high levels of aspiration and effort. Generations of repression and failure, along with a scarcity or absence of successful role models, make it difficult for the lower-class Negro student to see any potential rewards in educational efforts.

Aspiration level is also affected by one's knowledge of the performance of others. If information concerning the achievement of others is given to students before they know much about a subject, their levels of aspiration are influenced in the direction of what they know about the others' achievement. The aspirations and achievements of other children in the class are relevant factors in any single child's level of aspiration and expectation. Furthermore, many members of the community in which a lower-class student grows up have unclear, sometimes negative impressions of higher education. When the child grows up in such a community, he tends to adopt similar attitudes and does not aspire to do well in school. Bright children who go to school in neighborhoods where college is considered unimportant probably will not aspire to go beyond high school. On the other hand, a child who grows up in a neighborhood where he gets a chance to participate in a middle-class peer group may be highly motivated to go on in school. In lower-class neighborhoods teachers should spend time in the early grades on building higher levels of aspiration as part of their subject-matter planning.

## Achievement and Power Orientations

Middle-class children tend to develop strong desires to accomplish tasks well and to achieve. People from deprived backgrounds, on the other hand, tend to develop greater motivations to have influence and power over people. Evidently, experiences of being deprived and repressed are so frustrating that an unconscious wish or drive to dominate and command other people develops. Growing up with a sense of weakness leads to low expectations of being able to have influence and high incentives to wield power. The classroom is a situation in which some of this frustration and power motivation can be expressed. However, success in academic tasks occurs more often for people with strong achievement motivation. Youngsters with achievement orientations generally get satisfaction out of mastering a task, learning something, or doing well in something. Achievement motivation is supported and reinforced when the person sees himself mastering a challenge such as that presented by schoolwork. Power motivation, on the other hand, is reinforced only when the individual has been able to achieve influence control over the behaviors of another. Sometimes this is seen in the classroom when a deprived boy is not satisfied with mastering academic tasks because he has a strong unfulfilled wish for dominating the actions of the teacher or other students. When some of these wishes for influence are gratified, the lower-class male student might be able to do better on school tasks.

The emphasis on power orientations in the lower class is expressed by the way many lower-class people conceive of manliness. The lower-class boy learns that in order to become a male he must be aggressive, physically active, and sexually open. Moreover, both boys and girls of the lower class become aware of their sex-role patterns sooner than middle-class children. While lower-class boys tend to reach a stable pattern of sex identification by the time they are in kindergarten, middle-class boys do not do so until they are in the second grade. In the first grade, lower-class girls show clear knowledge and acceptance of their sex roles, but middle-class girls often do not even by the third grade.

There are several possible explanations for the earlier learnings of sex-appropriate behavior among lower-class children. Perhaps the customs, traditions, and taboos of their families provide early definitions and strong rewards for sex-appropriate behavior and severe punishment for sex-inappropriate behavior. Middle-class families may be more permissive in this respect and not as likely to punish masculine behavior in girls or feminine behavior in boys. It is also possible that adult masculine and feminine roles are more clearly differentiated in lower-class families; there are more tasks that are clearly either the father's or the mother's, and fewer that are shared by both. These parents may provide more clear-cut models of sex-appropriate behavior, thus facilitating youngsters' imitation of these responses.

The lower-class male's expression of aggressiveness and power sometimes develops because of an authoritarian father. In such homes the father's domination and control may have dammed up the impulses within the youngster. When the youngster gets into a neighborhood or school situation, he sometimes imitates the father's authoritarian approach.

The lower-class child also tends to have a strong fear of failure. He is often afraid that if he does not do something correctly, the same reaction he has received from an aggressive father, peer, or neighbor will occur in school. Authorities are viewed with mistrust; they have all too often deceived him in the past. The erratic behavior of the father in previous situations has shown the child that authorities are inconsistent and that their behavior cannot be predicted. The inconsistent behavior of the police in lower-class neighborhoods often reinforces the impression that one cannot trust authorities. The teacher is often seen as a similar authority who cannot be trusted. At the same time the youngster has a fear that if he does not go along with what the authorities are demanding, he will be severely punished. This combination of expectations often makes the lower-class student very ambivalent about authority and very uncomfortable in the presence of such figures.

# CHAPTER SIX

# Developing a Plan

Once the teacher has identified and clarified a problem situation and has diagnosed the state of affairs in his class, he is ready to consider appropriate plans of action. Since any classroom situation can be treated in a number of ways, the task of developing a plan is actually a matter of discovering and choosing among alternative courses of action.

After trying to improve their classroom situation, teachers are heard frequently to say, "Well, it didn't work. I didn't know if it would, but I thought I ought to try." Perhaps it didn't work because the teacher did not realize that moving from good intentions to successful practice requires careful planning, one of the most advanced skills of a truly professional worker. It is one thing, for instance, to be aware that a small group of pupils in the classroom have developed norms of resistance to learning, or that the academic achievements of some of the girls are undermining the boy's learning motivation. It is more difficult to make a plan to deal with these problems.

A number of personal as well as social barriers stand in the way of the teacher who wishes to develop a plan for action to deal with classroom problems. Developing plans to work on problems usually requires additional time and energy, and sometimes demands expertise and skill the teacher may feel he lacks. In addition to these personal feelings, sometimes colleague norms discourage communication and experimentation: when colleagues or principals reject or don't listen to new ideas, the teacher is likely to be less interested in actually proceeding with the development of a plan.

The teacher may develop a plan by himself, but even so he will find himself using various resources, among which will be his knowledge of the behavioral sciences, his sense of what is possible in his classroom, his familiarity with teaching techniques either used by teachers of his own acquaintance or discussed in educational texts and journals, and the suggestions of members of his class. The next two sections on deriving and sharing practices will discuss some ways in which teachers have availed themselves of these resources.

## Deriving a Plan

Ideally, when one has diagnosed a classroom problem, one should be able to apply a solution to it that has been extensively tested by others and that has a relatively sure chance of succeeding. Sometimes, however, it is rather difficult to discover research findings that address each specific classroom problem, and to locate solutions that have been tested out. The teacher often has to depend on his own experience, and thus it is important for him to know how to proceed from the diagnostic information to practices that will improve the learning atmosphere in his classroom.

The first major task in developing a plan from diagnostic data is to link each finding or explanation to a potential change activity. The sum of these change activities constitutes a plan for action. It is important not to simplify the dynamics of classroom behavior; most of the time the teacher will need to plan to change several influences at once.

However, even after he has made a sensitive identification of problems and a thorough diagnosis of the classroom learning environment, he may find that he cannot integrate the difficulties he is experiencing with his class into one problem to be treated. In the final analysis there may be two or more problems that have to be solved. In this case he will have to decide which problem is most crucial; he will have to assign an order of priority before he begins to make plans for change. For example, he may discover that peer group standards work to the detriment of academic achievement. Through diagnosis he may have learned that these standards are determined and enforced by a small group of classroom leaders. He may also learn that the students do not become involved in their studies because his own method of presentation is too verbal and conceptualized. In this case the solution of one problem will not lead to the solution of the other. The teacher may have definite ideas on how to approach the solution of each of these problems. He may plan to use the established peer leadership to form classroom steering committees having responsibility for setting standards of student behavior. He may also want to involve the students more in their studies through such methods as role playing and small work-project groups. Yet he will have to assign a priority to his innovation efforts. His attempts to use role playing and small work-project groups may well fail unless he first solves the problem of the antischool norms of the peer group leaders.

In the following case study of Mrs. Dome's classroom, the teacher proceeds from a review of diagnostic specifics to clear, concise, and well-thought-out designs for change. Not all teachers will plan as extensively as Mrs. Dome, but her designs are instructive in their continuity and potentiality for long-term success.

Mrs. Dome's students did not get along well with one another; they often fought on the school grounds and argued in class. After noting this fighting and arguing, Mrs. Dome reflected upon the timing and patterning of its occurrence. She became convinced that most of the fighting seemed to involve a few students who did not appear to have many friends in the class. These fighters seldom played with the other students and often seemed bored and withdrawn from games and activities. When at certain times they did ask to play, the other children refused their requests.

Mrs. Dome decided to administer a sociometric test that asked students who their friends were, whom they liked to play with and work with, and whom they didn't like being with. The conclusions she drew from these sociometric questions offered a possible explanation of the behavior she noticed. There were a few highly chosen and well-liked children, and a few who were often rejected. She realized that one result of this pattern was the operation of a peer circular process of rejection, somewhat like the teacher-student circular process described in Chapter Three. It started with one highly influential student rejecting a classmate and getting others to reject him also. Faced with such social ostracism, the rejectee took out his resentment against some of his peers by arguing and hitting. The student who was struck, along with his friends, rejected the aggressor even more strongly and the process went on and on. She knew that it was now up to her to change the cycle in some fashion and to establish a new cycle of positive relations. She had to develop some plan of action to alleviate or reverse the effects of these well-established patterns of interpersonal rejection and aggression.

She planned to change this situation by the use of several different teaching techniques. She decided to give special responsibility training to the highly liked students in order to teach them how to try to be understanding and patient with their peers. She also decided to meet simultaneously with some of the rejected pupils for discussions of classroom life and their role in it. She was concerned with teaching both the high- and low-status youngsters new skills in inclusion, acceptance, and support, along with asking for and responding to help. Finally she felt that for greatest success these activities would eventually have to be viewed by the students as just as important as, and intimately related to, subject-matter learning.

Mrs. Dome decided to use a special teaching procedure, which is a modification of role playing, called the auxiliary chair technique. A chair is used to represent a role or human characteristic such as effective or ineffective leadership or docile or aggressive behavior. The students are asked to project their feelings onto the chair and to attempt to understand how the chair would react. This technique provides both student and teacher with a simple form of role playing and, when followed by discussion, facilitates student understanding and appreciation of the causes of behavior. Finally, Mrs. Dome hoped that this procedure would dramatize a wide variety of behaviors and consequently be meaningful to most of the students.

After some time with this procedure Mrs. Dome felt she would be ready to try more intensive and formal training sessions. She planned to hold special sessions for the well-liked students in order to teach them how to encourage and reward acceptable behavior from rejected students. During such sessions the chair could be a supportive student, reaching out to include others. The students would discuss how the occupant of this chair would behave; they would then actually try out such behavior with one another and end up by evaluating their efforts.

Mrs. Dome also wished to train the socially ineffective students to work with and learn from their well-liked peers. In order to do this she planned to take her students into a kindergarten where they could observe other groups at work. She planned to have them observe these children to see which ones liked each other, which did not, and which were neutral. By recording and then discussing these observations, Mrs. Dome hoped that her second-graders gradually would become more sensitive observers of student interaction. However, these plans were not complete without some provision for more formal and continual training in human relations. Mrs. Dome felt that behavioral science, as subject matter and as problem-solving methodology, could be taught in weekly sessions at even the second-grade level. The content of these lessons might include working in small groups, making decisions, getting along with parents and siblings, and expressing positive and negative feelings. In each session she would use the auxiliary chair technique to dramatize the problem, would ask the students to record their observations and reactions, and would then discuss them. Then problem scenes could be reenacted, including some of the alternative responses that the students suggested in their discussion. Finally an attempt would be made to help the students apply the lessons learned from this particular unit to other aspects of their daily lives.

She felt at this point that she had a plan that was adequate to improve the negative atmosphere of the class. Further modifications and refinements of the plan were made by Mrs. Dome as she tried it out in the classroom. Her adaptation and action efforts, as well as her evaluation of the effects of the total plan, are described in Chapter Ten.

Mrs. Dome made use of her understanding of the circular pattern of peer rejection processes, but often a teacher, even after diagnosing the classroom situation, cannot put his finger on the behavioral-science explanations that are relevant to his problem. It would be wonderful, once the teacher has identified a professional problem, to be able to call up a "research retrieval center" and ask for all the relevant research that would be helpful in finding solutions. Some steps have been made in this direction in medical diagnosis and practice, and even greater steps in the field of the utilization of physical engineering knowledge. Professional education is still a long way from this ideal, but there are some sources of reference material that the teacher may find helpful. *Understanding Classroom Social Relations and Learning,* the volume upon which this booklet is based, contains much theoretical material and many research findings that a teacher might use to understand the underlying causes of classroom behavior. Berelson and Steiner have made an inventory of the present state of knowledge in the behavioral sciences.* Some of the more important behavioral science concepts and findings relevant to classroom problems have been reviewed briefly in Chapters Three and Five of this booklet. The following hypothetical illustration will focus on a teacher's use of a behavioral-science reference source as an aid in developing a plan.

Mrs. Olsen felt that some of her students were not receiving adequate parental support for their schoolwork. When the school held parent-teacher conferences very few of the parents of her students ever came to talk with her, and those that did made vague references to their attempts to "shape up my kid." From Chapter Five of this booklet she got the notion of a circular process of student failure and parental rejection of learning efforts. This seemed to fit her situation. For instance, the parents' lack of orientation to school success is perceived by the student, who as a result does not work hard in school. The student's subsequent lack of success causes the parents to feel even more negative toward the school, and toward the student as well. These increasingly negative attitudes are perceived and internalized by the student, who becomes even more apathetic and resistant in class.

Mrs. Olsen felt that this diagnosis was correct and tried to plan ways of intervening in the cycle. She derived several action implications:

1. Deal with parental rejection of learning efforts by more conferences, home visits, letters home, and the like.
2. Deal with student failure by guaranteeing success on small tasks.
3. Deal with the negative influence of the link between parental feelings and student motivation by examining it publicly and building alternative student supports.

She decided that the first procedure would take too much of her own time, and that the second might work to the detriment of some students

*Bernard Berelson and Gary A. Steiner, *Human Behavior: An Inventory of Scientific Findings* (New York: Harcourt, Brace & World, 1964).

who were working hard already. She decided to accept the third plan and develop it further. Mrs. Olsen designed a lesson on parental influences, which highlighted the ways in which parents and school can work together. Then she asked students to meet in small groups to share their perceptions of their parents' attitudes. It was her hope that these students would see parental support or nonsupport as a generational, not an individual, problem. Then she would be able to mobilize greater peer support in the classroom as a substitute for parental regard.

In addition to using his own resources to develop a plan for the classroom, the teacher can seek out and utilize the skills of social science or educational consultants. An illustration is the experience of Miss Arden, who felt quite dissatisfied with the motivation of some of her seventh-grade students. It seemed to her that usually there were a number of them sitting around scratching their heads because what was going on was beyond them, while a number of others were looking bored because things were moving so slowly. She administered a questionnaire asking the students how they felt about schoolwork, how hard they worked, how much they enjoyed the class, and the like. She discovered that about a quarter of the students felt unsuccessful and negative about the classroom activities and another quarter of them indicated they liked schoolwork moderately but didn't find things very exciting or interesting in her class session. Quite a number of students indicated they felt that they were not working very hard and that they were not going along with Miss Arden's suggestions.

Miss Arden decided to discuss the possible meaning of these findings with an educational consultant. The consultant looked at the questionnaire data and observed Miss Arden's class for a few hours. As they reviewed the data and talked over the events of a typical classroom session, they discussed several alternative plans for classroom change. One possibility involved Miss Arden's conferring with the most negative students; another possibility was her talking with their parents. It seemed clear that some students needed individual support to increase their learning motivation and their sense of responsibility for utilizing their own and the teacher's resources. To attempt this all by herself would require too much of Miss Arden's time and energy.

The consultant and Miss Arden thought through these energy allocation problems as well as their alternative ways of dealing with the data about her classroom. They emerged with a teaching design that involved a selection of about ten teaching aides from the most competent students and provided them with the challenge of working with one or two fellow students who were in need of tutorial help. The poorly achieving students responded very quickly to the help and support from their more competent peers, and the more advanced students were greatly stimulated by the opportunity and responsibility of being educational aides. In order to remain a member of the squad of educational aides, the advanced students were expected to do extra project work as well as to demonstrate proficiency as sensitive helpers of their peers. The design proved to be very effective because Miss Arden was motivated to carry on her own research and development process, and because with consultant help she was able to make a sound derivation from her data.

Sometimes the problems a teacher faces are not found solely in his classroom but may be common to an entire school or school system. In such cases, if principals and administrators agree, it is possible for an entire school system to utilize the various resources of the behavioral sciences to derive plans for improving the classroom learning atmosphere. An illustration of such a systemwide mobilization of resources in a derivation conference is presented below.

Some of the teachers and principals in an urban school system had become aware of a problem of acting-out behavior in upper elementary school boys, particularly in schools in underprivileged neighborhoods. A behavioral scientist was brought in as a consultant to run a derivation conference in order to gather research knowledge that would address the problem. He convened the concerned educators, as well as several colleagues in child development, social psychology, and sociology, to pool their knowledge about the problem. He posed the question, "What research findings or theoretical generalizations come to your mind that might be relevant to understanding some aspects of this problem of acting-out lower-class boys in upper elementary school classroom situations?" During a two-hour brainstorming session, twenty-five to thirty research generalizations were tentatively suggested as possibly relevant. Then the question was posed to the group, "What implications might these findings have for lines of action in attempting to help teachers and the students to solve this problem?"

At the end of this discussion period some of the statements of findings and of implications read as follows:

*Finding 1.* The negatively behaving child of nine to twelve years has often given up aspirations of competence in academic work and as a defense rejects the value of becoming successful in schoolwork.

> *Possible Implication:* Academic help will be rejected as meaningless unless evaluations about the self and about personal criteria of competence are raised.

*Finding 2.* Adult teachers have become rejected as definers of success experience and as models for identification.

45

> *Possible Implication:* Either a positive emotional relationship with a teacher will have to be established as a basis for redefining criteria of competence, or some other respected status figure, such as an older peer, will need to help in this redefining process.

*Finding 3.* These acting-out boys tend to be rejected sociometrically and to feel rejected by the proschool and proteacher peers and to form an antiteacher and antischool subgroup.

> *Possible Implication:* Acceptance by and integration into the proschool peer culture should be a major objective, especially through work with academically effective peer leaders.

Many such connections between research generalizations and implication statements were made during the forenoon conference. The scientists found it handy to refer to research volumes during the brainstorming process.

The next step in this process was to ask, "What kind of design for action is suggested by these implication statements?" Out of this effort to link implication statements with action ideas came the type of derivations illustrated by the chart on page 47. The eight designs for action are connected with one or more of the implication statements.

From these designs for action a program was initiated, along with a plan for its evaluation. Several modifications were made as feedback came in from the evaluation, but on the whole the design proved quite successful in helping the teachers develop a practice that substantially improved this particular educational problem. At first glance, this may seem to be an overly complicated process for improving educational practice. Actually it is a very modest and in many ways inadequate effort compared with the importance of the educational problem—the development of procedures for helping an appreciable number of young boys to become identified with the academic learning process and to begin to move along the track of healthy growth and development.

This approach to pooling relevant knowledge and deriving ideas and designs for new practice requires that someone in the school system be prepared to bring into the schools a resource consultant or consultants from the outside. This change agent (or linking person) might be in the central administration or a principal or a committee of teachers. Moreover, initiative might be taken by a building staff to request a professional seminar on a series of topics they have defined as requiring knowledge retrieval and suggestions for action. Many of the topics suggested in Chapters Three and Five could be the basis for such a series of discussions, with invited experts participating in a program that would present readings on recent research and theory.

| Implications from Research Findings | Action Design for Implementation |
|---|---|
| 1. Need to experience a positive relationship with a teacher. | 1. Special classroom<br>—8 students together for a half day<br>—focus on academic fundamentals and behavioral interaction<br>—weekly training consultant for teacher |
| 2. Change in values of self and of competence needs to precede acceptance of school subjects. | |
| 3. Project-oriented school experiences are most likely to provide necessary success in initial approach with academic work. | 2. Visiting teacher<br>—meets weekly with each child<br>—meets weekly with parents of child |
| 4. Need acceptance by, and integration into, the socialized peer culture. | 3. Regular classroom human relations training<br>—consultant - demonstrator works in same classroom<br>—teachers and consultant meet weekly as a resource team on problem solving and developing classroom innovations |
| 5. Individual values and norms are best modified by proteacher, proschool peers. | |
| 6. Work with parents on relations with the child and the school should result in improved school adjustment of the child. | 4. Afterschool activities clubs<br>— antischool students with proschool peers<br>—consultant - demonstrator leads some clubs<br>—consultant meets weekly with adult leader |
| 7. Work with child on relations with parents should improve school adjustment. | |
| 8. Rewarding contacts with community authority figures should yield improved school adjustment. | 5. Child in regular school program half day |
| | 6. Case conferences<br>—semimonthly for involved school staff and clinicians |
| 9. Interesting projects need to be planned providing basic skill practice and success experience for self-reevaluation. | 7. Policy committee meetings<br>—annual meeting for evaluative reporting and policy review<br>All seven above |
| 10. Continuity of regular school program should be maintained. | 8. Evaluation team<br>—action-research team relates to program personnel as indicated above<br>—conducts data analysis and reports results |
| 11. Multiple-entry approach of programing in several areas should be applied. | |

47

## Sharing Plans

Clearly one of the easiest ways a teacher can learn about different teaching methods that might improve his classroom situation is to take advantage of the experiences of other teachers. Every year dedicated, creative teachers invent hundreds of new teaching practices to cope with specific educational problems they find themselves facing. Of course many of these inventions are unsuccessful and should be discontinued. Many times, however, teaching inventions are successful in coping with important educational problems and should become available to fellow practitioners, but do not. This is a tremendous loss of professional expertise, and this section will discuss some of the ways that such expertise can be shared by teachers.

What are the reasons that teachers do not communicate or share some of their successful innovative plans and practices with colleagues? Many times the teacher does not know his practice is new or potentially useful to others, and feels inhibited about blowing his own horn with his colleagues. Also colleagues are somewhat hesitant to ask about a practice, if they have heard about it, because many teachers have the unfortunate idea that to imitate somebody else would be viewed as evidence of their own lack of creativity and adequacy. If a practice is shared with colleagues, typically the communication is so incomplete that a teacher would have great difficulty successfully adopting or adapting the plan. Often the innovator cannot adequately document or report what he has done to make it useful to others.

Clearly some organized and disciplined process of sharing is one of the most effective ways in which a teacher, searching for solutions to his own particular problems, can find possible designs for action that are relevant to his classroom. How can teachers initiate and utilize a systematic sharing process? A brief write-up of a teaching practice, in a professional journal or a local school system newsletter, does not provide all the needed information, does not necessarily locate the most important practices, and does not provide support for tryout of the new ideas and techniques. Furthermore, information is often missing that would help the teacher understand why and how the invention might not have worked and under what conditions it should be discontinued.

Perhaps one of the most important aids to developing a plan for action is adequate documentation of how the other person did it so that it is possible to understand the major steps of action and the key skill points involved in the performance. The teacher who wishes to use the experience of his colleagues must be prepared to do more than just passively receive the account of a successful experience. He must have a clear idea of the problem in his classroom and perhaps a tentative plan of his own that he can discuss with his colleagues. Further, he must dig for information that can make the link between the innovator's experience and his own class. Finally, he must set priorities of change efforts and plan to use a practice that most effectively moves toward his classroom goals. The following example will show how a teacher can make use of the valuable resources of an experienced colleague.

Miss Ames had been very stimulated by hearing Mrs. Brown, a sixth-grade teacher, talk about her class during a coffee hour. Mrs. Brown was discussing her use of a classroom steering committee. Evidently, four students served as a steering committee to lead the class in establishing rules of behavior in the classroom and then helped evaluate how well the rules were being observed each day. This seemed a simple enough idea and Miss Ames decided she would like to try it.

As she thought about it that evening, several questions came to mind. She decided she had better talk more fully with Mrs. Brown about the procedures that she had found worked best in using this steering committee. In conversation with Mrs. Brown at the end of school the next day, she discovered that Mrs. Brown had used a sociometric questionnaire to identify influential opinion leaders in the classroom, and also to identify those who felt negative or positive about schoolwork and classroom activities. On the basis of these diagnostic data, Mrs. Brown had been able to appoint an initial steering committee made up of influential leaders who were a mixture of both the proschool and antischool factions of the classroom.

Next she discovered that Mrs. Brown not only delegated responsibility to the steering committee, but provided the members with initial and continuing consultation so that their efforts would be rewarding and helpful to the class. She met with them at the noon hour to help them plan their leadership of classroom sessions, to decide what they would look for in observations, and to discuss such important strategies as looking for and reporting positive things in the class as well as making critical remarks. In fact, Miss Ames became aware that there were some real traps in this process of observations and evaluation of classroom activities by the steering committee unless the total classroom group understood what was going on, and unless the steering committee did a sensitive and positive job in their observation and reporting.

Miss Ames was pleased when Mrs. Brown invited her to sit in on a noon meeting of the steering committee so that she could get a more concrete idea of what was going on. As she sat and listened at the next weekly meeting of the steering committee, Miss Ames realized that Mrs. Brown was demonstrating some very important skills in stimulating active creative thinking on the part of the pupils without dominating them, and at the same time she was providing genuine resource ideas that would help

49

the youngsters gain a meaningful perspective on what they were doing. Miss Ames also learned at this meeting that each steering committee served for three weeks and then appointed four successors to take on the job for the next three weeks, with no one being reappointed until everyone in the room had served.

Miss Ames later realized that she had not asked Mrs. Brown's advice on whether there were certain things she would do differently if she were starting again. Mrs. Brown was challenged by the questions and after reflecting a bit said, "I think the thing I am most dubious about is having the whole steering committee turning over at one time. I think maybe there ought to be some old-timers to help the new ones get oriented so they would be less dependent on me."

As Miss Ames thought about the difference between the age and maturity of her group and Mrs. Brown's class, two adaptations seemed relevant to her. One was for her to take more initial responsibility in getting the total class to think about the symptoms of effective and ineffective classroom life so that the steering committee would have more guidance in their observation and more support from the classroom group in their discussions. The second adaptation that seemed appropriate to her was to introduce a weekly classroom election of the two new steering committee members so that the whole class could be involved in sanctioning and supporting their representatives.

This illustration shows that utilizing the creative teaching practice of a colleague is not a simple process. What a teacher is adopting and adapting is a complex behavior pattern involving values, concepts, and skills. Usually his personal style of teaching and his classroom group require that he modify and refine the new practice for his own use. Chapter Eight will discuss at greater length the process of adapting a teaching plan to the peculiarities of one's own classroom.

In sharing, as in deriving, a school or school system can facilitate the development of new techniques to improve the classroom learning atmosphere. Sometimes the administration can free teacher time and energy for sharing ideas and developing new teaching programs. One such example is found in the experience of teachers in leaving their own classroom to observe another teacher or to visit another building where an exciting and relevant plan had been developed. In going to observe another teacher in action, it is best to know ahead of time what one is looking for.

After the observation the visiting teacher can use a tape recorder to interview the demonstrating teacher on how he planned and what were the key elements of his practice. The tape is then available as a piece of documentary material for the other teachers. It would be quite feasible for a school building or a school system to develop a library of documentary tapes of systematic interviews with teachers about their practices.

Another systemwide facilitating activity that can be illustrated is a methodical search for promising plans and practices. In one school system a one-page questionnaire was developed asking each teacher to nominate, with a brief description, any promising practice he himself had used, or knew a colleague had used. These were defined as practices he felt were somewhat different from what most teachers did and seemed successful in stimulating students to learn. He was asked to describe the practice, discuss resources required for using it, state the goals he was working toward, review what happened while trying out the practice, and finally to evaluate the success of the practice.

These questionnaires were distributed by a committee in each school system composed of a central administrator, elementary and secondary school principals, and three or four teachers from different schools and classroom levels. Over three hundred nominations were received, and the next important step was getting help from a consulting behavioral scientist and educational psychologist to work along with the committee in screening the practices for the ones that ought to be followed up for more intensive documentation. They used a number of ratings—for example, how consistent the practice was with educational research and theory; how applicable to a variety of classroom settings; how difficult or easy to adopt. Ten selection criteria were developed and thirty practices were selected for intensive description. The write-ups were distributed through the school system and opportunities were provided for teachers to consider them, decide whether they wanted to explore any of them seriously, and then to receive the consultant help of another teacher or an outside resource person if they wanted to try out the new practice. In many cases two or three teachers working together supported each other in trying out and adapting a new practice to their own teaching styles and classroom groups.

# CHAPTER SEVEN

# Teaching Practices to Improve the Classroom Atmosphere

This chapter will discuss some practices that teachers have found helpful in improving student self-esteem, peer relations and norms, and teacher-student relations. The chapter will be divided into three sections and will consider some general properties of the practices of forming small work-project groups, of involving students in subject-matter planning and presentation, and of forming student governments in the classroom. The discussion in these sections is meant to be merely suggestive, and does not pretend to exhaust the many variations and modifications of these practices that teachers have used. It will have served its purpose if it can stimulate the teacher in the problem-solving phases of planning, adaptation, and action. Thus, this chapter is an interlude in the discussion of the phases, and can be used by the teacher as a resource of possible plans.

## Small Work Groups

Forming the class into small work groups is often useful for improving the classroom learning atmosphere. Such groups can be used to fulfill a variety of aims: establish tutoring relationships, reinforce friendly relations, teach task collaboration, enhance achievement, and so on. The basis on which the teacher sets up the groups will vary with his aim.

### Criteria for Forming Work Groups

Five criteria for grouping will be briefly discussed here. The first two types of grouping will be those in which the members complement each other either academically or interpersonally. The last three are those that are formed on the basis of something the members have in common.

Complementarity might be the basis for grouping when some students have been neglected or rejected by their peers. With sociometric test results the teacher can identify the actual or potential friends of low-peer-status students. If the teacher is unable to locate any friend for a student, he might place him in a group with students receiving many positive choices, because such students are probably quite secure and able to support the rejected or neglected student. The neglected student also may be able to learn new behaviors by observing these socially effective classmates.

Grouping might also be based on mutual academic needs through peer tutoring groups. Sometimes the teacher finds that he has some competent students who do not respect others or who are often disruptive and disturbing to others. At the same time there may be many other students who do not perform well in certain subjects. Both parties can be helped sometimes by tutoring relationships in which the more competent students are asked to assist the less able ones. Such relationships have been shown to improve the academic interest and competence of the slower students and help the competent ones become more responsible and diligent in their own work.

Common interest often is the best method of grouping when classroom projects are carried out. Such assignments as reporting on a country, preparing a historical mural, making a model, and working on a classroom newspaper are examples of academic work that can be facilitated by grouping for common interests.

Teachers might group according to ability levels, especially if some students are frustrated by comparing their work with that of more competent peers. Some teachers have established ability groups in which the students are expected to check each other's papers and help each other with the mistakes. In such classrooms students often are left free to move from one ability group to another as they feel their work is becoming too difficult or too easy.

A final basis for grouping is that of friendship. One method of going about this is to use a sociometric questionnaire asking the students with whom they would like to work. If the classroom social structure is well diffused, this method will work. However, if it is not—if there are one or two small clusters of highly chosen students, with the rest of the class members being mere followers—the teacher may be advised to try another method, such as having the students elect group leaders who in turn would select group members, much as children choose up sides in a sandlot baseball game. This procedure has the disadvantage of publicly exposing the least desirable members of the class, those who are chosen last; however, the leaders, or captains, could do their selecting in private, and then the group formations could be publicly announced. If a teacher uses a method such as this, he should instruct the leaders to make sure all members of the team are fruitfully involved in the work project, and not to display favoritism toward any one or two of his close friends. If the teacher does not trust the class to elect captains who are bright or serious enough to function effectively as leaders, the teacher may ask the

53

students to elect, for example, six captains from whom he would pick three.

Occasionally a teacher might choose the criterion of friendship because he can think of no other way to get the students to work together in small groups. The two methods of grouping on the criteria of friendship—that of having the students select their workmates in a sociometrically diffused class and that of having the stars choose groups in a more hierarchical class—share the limitation that popularity is the major issue. The teacher can try to shift the focus by the following method.

He might give team captains the option of sharing members with another team—just as a baseball team with two good shortstops might want to trade one for a good pitcher. A classroom team working on a project that required the construction of maps, charts, or drawings might have two good artists and need someone skilled in another aspect of the project, say a student who enjoyed writing or one who had a special enthusiasm for the subject matter of the project. In this way the entire class could be led to see the diversity of talents among its members, and begin to value each other for their talents. It would be best, though, that the teacher act as the clearinghouse for all trades to ensure that the teams are trading skills and not personalities, and that those who are traded realize that they are moving because they have a talent that someone else needs.

### Preparing the Class to Work in Small Groups

The care with which the teacher selects the criterion for forming the groups will greatly determine their success. Even with the most skillful formation of groups, however, they may still fail if the students have not had much experience of this sort.

In many cases it is advisable for the teacher to prepare the class for group work. Role-playing methods have been used with success to help students learn how to work in groups. One teacher used role playing in the following way: Four students chosen on the basis of their high peer status and cooperation in the classroom were asked to present two improvisations. These students took different parts: one was the chairman, while the others were a child with many ideas, most of which were not well thought through; a child with high intelligence who liked to work alone; and a child prone to goof off, play around, and work badly in the group.

This committee was supposed to work on a report of how it would be to live in South America today. For the first exercise the chairman was briefed to be bossy and controlling. He was also supposed to be very critical of others. The students enacted the drama for the class, and the work on the report was very poor. Then the second exercise was done and the chairman was told to try to get everybody's ideas while encouraging full participation; this session worked much better.

A discussion was conducted after the session about the various roles played and "how many of us are like the people depicted in the play." The next full session involved multiple role playing in which the class was divided into six groups; three were role-playing groups while three were observing. Each role-playing group was paired with an observing group, and these pairs went off into different corners of the room. Each tried to enact a good group discussion using what they had learned the preceding day. Discussions ensued once more on "What makes us able or not able to work effectively together?" Finally a third session was held during which different groups of students attempted to enact model groups for future work. Discussion followed and the students summarized what they had learned.*

Even two-student tutoring relationships are usually not successful unless the teacher gives training to both students. Such training can take the form of classroom demonstration in which several students are asked to act out what they would consider an effective tutoring relationship, and several others to depict an ineffective relationship. A classroom discussion should follow in which the teacher can encourage and instruct the class to follow the effective tutoring pattern.

The teacher may want to give special leadership training to the team leaders or chairmen. One of the advantages of having class members engaged in group projects is that it gives members responsibility for the accuracy and completion of their assignments. The teacher might meet with one group daily, mainly to introduce new work; of course he can be approached for special assistance, but the groups will generally be responsible for producing their own work. Such a situation will work only if the members of the groups can get along with each other. Through role playing, the class may have learned the differences between a productive and an unproductive group, but effective leadership is still indispensable to good group functioning; the group chairman or leader must be responsive to the needs of individual members. The technique of having leaders chosen by the class rather than by the teacher does not necessarily mean that they will be any more responsive to the needs of team members for personal support.

Each grouping pattern is limited in usefulness and to be used only tentatively. The grouping and regrouping of students is often more significant than the criterion the teacher uses, because youngsters tend to be stimulated by changing classroom experiences. Positive classroom atmos-

---

*A detailed discussion of how best to conduct role-playing sessions such as these can be found in the booklet *Role-Playing Methods in the Classroom.*

pheres sometimes are facilitated by frequent experimenting with new groupings and seating arrangements. The new practice, whatever it is, lends a feeling to the students that the teacher thinks they are important and that he is trying these new arrangements to improve the classroom. Constant regrouping also helps avoid permanent and rigid cliques or "tracks" in the classroom. When different students work together on many different tasks, informal barriers can be broken down, and students may work better. Feedback discussion, as proposed in Chapter Nine, should be held periodically to see how the students are reacting to the various grouping patterns.

## Subject-Matter Planning and Presentation by Students

Sometimes students find it difficult to learn academic subjects taught in traditional styles. They have little internal drive to learn, and pushing fails to get them deeply involved; they are uninterested and bored. Some teachers have attempted to change student attitudes like these by trying teaching designs that encourage emotional and behavioral as well as cognitive participation.

Students tend to work harder and learn more when they have chosen and structured tasks themselves. Sometimes student involvement in subject planning frees the teacher to give more careful attention to students with special learning needs. Also the classroom atmosphere tends to be improved because of the feelings of commitment to learning generated by involvement. Consequently many teachers attempt to increase academic interest and achievement by encouraging greater student participation in some stages of subject-matter planning and presentation. At all times, however, the teacher will retain his principal professional responsibility for curriculum determination.

One of the most frequently used practices is giving students an opportunity to teach their own lesson plans. This approach can combine student teaching with the interest or ability grouping described in the last section. The teacher first forms study groups, outlines the responsibilities of what a leader would do in each group, and asks leaders to submit lesson plans generated by the group. These are reviewed by the teacher, then given back to the groups with recommendations for improvement, and a revised plan is submitted by each group until it is accepted by the teacher. Each group then sets out to execute its plan.

In a simpler variation of student planning, the teacher determines the general topic, allowing the students to plan the ways in which they will proceed with the topic; different interest and ability groups might study the topic from various points of view. Later, class reports can be made and the total topic put together in a final product, perhaps as a

56

class newspaper or booklet, a play or a show with different acts, or a series of presentations. Another possibility is a panel discussion in which representatives of each group contribute what their group has learned about the topic studied.

The teacher should anticipate that students often set unrealistic goals for themselves. They will set objectives too high more often than too low, and the experience of not being able to reach their goals will frustrate them. Often student goals will also be vague; in fact, unrealistically high and vague goals often accompany each other. The teacher should then be sure that the plans submitted to him have goals that are both specific and attainable with the material and intellectual resources available to the students.

An aid to the student groups that are drawing up plans would be an outline or a checklist prepared by the teacher and submitted to the groups beforehand. A typical checklist might be as follows:

Material resources needed
—Are they already available in class?
—Can they be brought to class by any of the students? By whom?
—Can they be constructed in class? By whom?
—Can they be obtained by the teacher? How?

Intellectual resources (knowledge) needed
—Does the class as a whole need to have special knowledge as background?
—Where will the knowledge be obtained? What books? What pictures?
—What members of the class have these resources?
—What members of the class should obtain these resources?
—Should the teacher's knowledge of the subject be used or relied on?
—Will an "expert" be brought in? Who? How?

Skills or talents needed
—What skills are needed?
—Who in the class has these skills?
—Are they skills or talents that will be developed? How?
—Are the teacher's skills to be used?

Sequence of action
—What is the major goal of the project?
—Do some parts of the project have to be completed before others can begin? Which ones come first?
—Are all parts of the project equally essential? If difficulties arise, which parts of the project can be dropped without ruining the whole? Which are most expendable?

57

—How rigid should the time schedule be? How rigid does it have to be? Can the project be completed within the year, semester, or month, (or whatever unit of time the teacher wishes to use)?

This checklist is of course merely suggestive; the teacher might want to modify it in any of several directions. He may, for example, first want the study groups to submit a plan before he gives them a checklist. In this case the checklist would ask more specific questions, questions addressed particularly to the proposed plan. Finally, the complexity and sophistication of the checklist a teacher will want to use will depend on the maturity and experience of his class. Another variation is to ask the project groups to submit their own checklists.

Often teachers will want to involve students more actively in the presentation of subject matter without demanding so much from them in the way of planning. A teacher may judge that his students are not capable of planning and carrying out a work project. One method of raising student involvement for these teachers might be to use role playing, which involves students motorically and emotionally in the learning process and is especially useful with lower-class children. The interested teacher should consult the booklet *Role-Playing Methods in the Classroom*.

One teacher used student dramatic presentation to raise interest in American history. He had started a discussion on the various areas of the United States that the students had lived in or visited. It was discovered that life in America today does not vary greatly from one area to another. By contrast, he pointed out that early Americans living in different locations would have led lives vastly different from others living at the same time in different parts of the country.

The class decided to present three plays to demonstrate these differences. The teacher used the class alphabetical list and divided it into three groups. Each group chose a chairman to lead the discussion in an orderly fashion and a secretary to keep a record of decisions. Several students in each group volunteered to write the script for the group based on ideas presented by members of the group. When the scripts were finished, each group chose the one they thought was best. The plays were dittoed by the teacher, and each child was given a copy and assigned a part in the play.

Each group worked on its own play and practiced in different parts of the room without teacher help. When they felt competent enough, each group presented its play to the other members of the class. This practice period lasted four days and was followed by formal presentations in the auditorium for other classes.

Another method of increasing student involvement is through excursions in which the students have the responsibility of collecting data of some sort. One teacher attempted to teach his students social studies by first training them to conduct interviews about community activities. One group of these students then interviewed the school principal and school board members; another group spoke with the mayor and city councilmen. During municipal elections the teacher encouraged the students to join the campaign for the candidate or party of their choice. For all these excursions the teacher helped the students establish contacts and make appointments. After these experiences the students shared their new insights and knowledge about their own community, and about community processes in general, with the rest of the class.

### Building an Atmosphere Conducive to Active Student Participation

Because of peer-group relations and norms, or because of longstanding habits of apathy in the classroom, students may resist efforts designed to bring them more actively into the learning process. The teacher who meets or anticipates this resistance is wise to try to form a classroom atmosphere that will encourage and support active student participation in classroom activities.

In general, there are two ways that the teacher can do this, and often it is advisable to use both at the same time. The first aims at encouraging more interpersonal acceptance among the students, and the second encourages student evaluation of classroom activities and the teacher's methods.

The teacher can emphasize the importance of recognizing and respecting individual differences among the students. Positive acceptance of differences is supportive in that it allows students to be respected for being themselves and does not force superficial conformity. Sometimes behavior that heretofore was described as "oddball" or "peculiar" can then become "unique" and "interesting." In one method for encouraging acceptance of individual differences, the teacher can collect questionnaire data from the students on their special talents and interests. He can then prepare a chart placing their skills and hobbies next to their names. Sometimes students are surprised to find that people stereotyped as enemies are quite similar to them or have some very unique and interesting hobby. Such discoveries can be encouraged by a teacher's also exposing some of his own talents and hobbies.

Another method of encouraging peer acquaintance and emotional support is to have each student interview one of his classmates in order to gather pertinent material for use in a classroom biography. After a biography for each student in the room is completed, the class can play the game of "Guess Who" or "I've Got a Secret." During the game the students try to identify the person described in the biography and in the process learn something about each child's background, likes and dislikes, interests, hobbies, strengths and weaknesses. Every child has the entire group's interest and attention focused on his life before his identity is divulged. Later the students may prepare a class biography.

In trying to build a classroom that encourages students to participate actively, the teacher should also permit and stimulate open discussion of his methods and of classroom activities in general. It is not always easy to get students to participate in these discussions, however, and the teacher may want to study the section in Chapter Nine on building an open communications atmosphere. The importance of open, mutual evaluation of the classroom atmosphere cannot be denied. The more open and forthright the teacher is about his goals, the more likely it is that the students will feel free to enter into classroom activities. Perhaps most importantly, communication from teacher to students and from students to teacher may help the students understand how their attitude toward school affects their ability to learn. Thus students who have been performing poorly may be saved from the damaging image of themselves as inadequate. If a student can see that his inability to learn is often caused by certain things that the teacher or other students do in his classroom, he may learn a more relaxed and confident approach to his own abilities. If the teacher is secure enough to draw out and react to feedback from his students, he may be able to present to them several caricatures of unsuccessful teacher styles such as "the long-winded bore," "the fault-finder," and "the peddler of shoddy goods." Thus the students can view the teacher with a more human perspective, and see that day-to-day failures are in many cases failures in human interaction rather than the inevitable result of teacher contrariness or student inadequacy.

In one method of initiating student evaluation, the students can be asked to write short essays on the topic of good and bad days in the classroom. They can be told that they should assume the role of a detective searching for clues as to what makes a day in class good or bad. The teacher then may review the essays and read the most relevant aloud to the class, or he may want to let the students read their own essays aloud. Class discussions can then focus on what can be done to make the classroom a better place in which to learn.

## Student Government for Maintaining Classroom Discipline

When students take part in formulating classroom rules and regulations about behavior, they are likely to act in a more responsible fashion to these rules than if the rules are made up and enforced by the teacher.

Not only are students likely to follow rules they make themselves, but a sense of control or power in the classroom may also contribute to academic achievement. Various methods for building a classroom student government have been employed; all of them involve the teacher in the role of guide and enabler, and occasionally as veto agent. It is important that the teacher not take an extremely active role in formulating rules, because this lessens the opportunity for student contribution. Yet he is usually available as a consultant in developing student skill and as a final arbiter in evaluating student decisions.

One technique for the development of a classroom government is a steering committee made up of a small group of sociometrically derived or elected leaders who meet occasionally with the teacher to suggest new rules for classroom operation. The steering committee acts as a group of class representatives that creates new laws and procedures for the entire group to consider. Usually a majority vote is needed by the class before a new rule is considered binding. Sometimes the teacher may have to initiate a debate by supporting the minority point of view just so that the class is not easily influenced by the majority. Once the first steering committee has gotten things started, rotation is advisable. Each steering committee chooses a new group, which in turn chooses another, until all students in the class have served as members. In this way many students have the opportunity to fulfill the leadership roles. The class also decides on appropriate punishments for breaking the rules, although the teacher usually should encourage an understanding of the causes behind breaking class rules. He should also encourage working for ways to improve classroom conditions without meting out punishment. Through this practice the students can learn about group decision making and government, as well as improve the classroom learning environment.

A different approach can be illustrated by the methods used in one classroom. Early in the year the class voted for a rules committee. The teacher met with this committee to help them think about what rules are, what would be good rules, and how class members could be involved in making and observing rules. This committee set up a bill of rights for all students and presented it to the class for discussion and approval. The class voted to accept the code after suggesting several minor changes. The following are examples of the rights: (1) People have a right to hear, so let them. (2) People have a right to talk, so don't interrupt a speaker— wait your turn. (3) Student behavior outside the classroom reflects upon the class and students in it. (4) Responsibility comes with office—lack of regard for school rules may result in removal from office.

The class was wary of giving too much authority to any one group and decided to form a separate committee to enforce rules. They voted for a judiciary committee consisting of two boys and two girls. At first these students were in office for two weeks, but they found this unsatisfactory because it did not allow enough time to learn the responsibilities for a fair and honest job. The class voted to extend the term of office to four weeks.

Daily the judiciary committee put a schedule of that day's activities on the board, including the name of the committee member who would be responsible for supervision of behavior during each part of the day. A system of "citizen's arrest" was also proposed, but it was seldom used. Under this system any child could draw up a slip saying someone was bothering him or misbehaving in a way that upset him, have it witnessed by another citizen, and submit it to the committee for action. The judiciary committee and the class officers also met as a group to rearrange the class seating plans as necessary.

Typically things do not go smoothly during initiation and organization of a classroom government. There are usually arguments and disruptions, especially at the beginning of the plan, and these must be taken in stride. Resistance, apathy, and lack of skill are among the major stumbling blocks. However, the potential benefits far outweigh these disadvantages. Through the participation and involvement of students in managing classroom discipline, the teacher is able to spend much more time on academic and intellectual development. Furthermore the youngsters are learning some very important skills in governing themselves.

Yet, if the teacher anticipates or meets too much resistance or apathy, he may want to try to prepare the class more gradually for the management of their own behavior. One method that was used by a teacher was to open the class to human relations discussions. At first he used short stories and had the youngsters act out the roles of various characters. The children gradually developed a relaxed feeling about discussing human relations and exposing their feelings before the class. Later, when a child had a personal problem that might be discussed in the class, the teacher encouraged the class to talk about it. All children were supported in their expressions of feelings and in the explorations of the reasons for these feelings. Many times students were also asked to make suggestions to improve the situation. In some instances, students discussed problems in classroom life. When this happened, the teacher would have a meeting with one or two of the class leaders to have them help in the solution of the problem. Students received support from their peers for attempts to improve classroom conditions, but these attempts at change usually had more impact if the whole class was involved in discussing them.

# CHAPTER EIGHT

# *Adaptation and Action*

The next major phase, involving some of the most important and least understood barriers to successful problem solving, is adapting a teaching plan to one's own classroom needs and personal resources, and then trying it out. The best preparation for this phase is thorough diagnosis and planning; yet even with the information gleaned from prior phases the teacher must think creatively about adapting a plan to his own teaching style, students, and classroom group, and about exercising the behavior skills necessary for carrying out the new practice. The following two sections will discuss these steps of adaptation and action.

## *The Adaptation Process*

Frequently teachers don't use an exciting practice because they don't see, or haven't tried to see, how it might be changed slightly to fit their own classroom. Just as often, enthusiastic teachers plunge ahead with a new teaching practice without adequate modification of it for their own situation. The reason for the ensuing disappointment is often not that the idea doesn't have real merits, but that there has been no thorough mastering of the idea and appropriate modification for the particular class and personal style of teaching. Utilizing the professional practices developed by one's colleagues is in itself a creative professional skill. It is certainly not just the simple matter of imitation that many teachers seem to think it is and consequently reject with a sense of pride in their professional self-sufficiency. Many teachers describe how they get a sense of satisfaction or completion out of "being up on the new ideas" through reading or attendance at professional meetings, and this satisfaction can often become a substitute for the more difficult but exciting step of moving into the adaptation of the idea to one's own classroom. Adaptation is a critical step in the problem-solving process because—

1. *Teachers differ in their values, personalities, and teaching styles, and each is more effective and comfortable with his own particular practices.*

Teachers who have different values about socialization and educational processes will identify different classroom problems as needing work. Similarly, they will adapt different plans to deal with these problems. For some teachers, problems of student irresponsibility are best met with punishment, while for others reward seems most appropriate. The disagreement here may not be on what's "most effective," but what's "right." It is partly on the basis of values as well as that of effectiveness that teachers set priorities for different actions. An example occurs often in adapting grouping procedures to one's own class. Some teachers feel friendship is irrelevant in the classroom and so will not group on this basis, regardless of the data.

Adaptation might be influenced by the teacher's personality, for example, if the teacher found that he had a special talent for playing certain roles, and that by participating with his students in the role play as an actor he could stimulate them to freer and more creative expression. Other teachers, however, would prefer to have students play all the roles in the drama, and limit their own function to giving advice and encouragement.

In working with classroom steering committees, too, teachers will establish different working arrangements with the student groups. Some teachers prefer to participate in such groups with no special rights, others prefer to limit the discussion to certain topics, and still others prefer to reserve for themselves the right of veto.

2. *Student characteristics such as age, social class, and personality differ from class to class.*

Chapter Five discussed some of the important implications of social class for teacher planning. A teacher who decided to use the practice of having students prepare arguments and debate them with other students in front of the class would follow a different procedure with middle-class youngsters, who were constantly exposed to verbal competition in their homes, from that with lower-class youngsters whose home and neighborhood methods of communication were usually more physical than verbal. Middle-class youngsters may be comfortable with conceptual descriptions, whereas it might be well to advise lower-class youngsters to act out the examples they use to support their arguments.

A teacher who reads about a teaching practice of dividing the class into small work groups may upon reflection realize that in the classroom that was described most of the youngsters had strong needs for achievement; that is, that they probably came from homes where the need for achievement and mastery of subject matter was emphasized. He may realize that his youngsters are different, that they seem to have more of a need to exercise power over each other regardless of whether or not any academic progress is being made. This teacher should not expect the same results or difficulties with the practice, and he should modify it for use in his classroom.

As we saw in Chapter Six, Miss Ames modified the teaching practice of a steering committee developed by Mrs. Brown because of the differences in age and maturity between the two groups. She decided to take more responsibility than Mrs. Brown had taken for guiding and sanctioning the activities of the steering committee. Because of her concern that some of the students might become overly dominating, she tried to give the whole class sanctioning power by having them elect new steering committee members every two weeks.

3. *Classroom peer groups differ in their social relations and norms.*

Another teacher started with the general plan of establishing "helping clusters" in which one or two high-achieving students would work with three or four less advanced students. He realized that the plan should be adapted to the hierarchical influence structure of his classroom group, and began by convening a small group of the most influential peers.

From their reactions, it was clear that the students wanted to be given the opportunity to indicate whom they would like to be grouped with as helpers, rather than let the teacher do the grouping. As one of them put it, "Some of the kids that are good at doing things I don't like very much, and others I like a lot. I think I could learn better if I liked our group leader some."

Another suggestion that came from the group of students was that the students selected to be helpers should not necessarily be a permanent team, but that others should be given the chance if they showed progress. These and other ideas led this teacher to refine his initial plan quite a bit before he met with the classroom group. He also felt much more at ease in his discussion with the whole class about the plan because he had the support of the key members of the class. With a less hierarchical peer group, he might have presented the general plan for total class discussion from the beginning.

Because of the three clusters of variables listed above, teachers will differ in their goal priorities. For example, as we saw in the last chapter, small work-project groups can be used to fulfill a variety of aims. The teacher's aim will determine how he sets up these work groups and the tasks he assigns them. The question of priority was considered in the section on developing a plan; but it may be well for the teacher to consider it once again when he is adapting the plan to his class: he may have to make further distinctions of priority on the basis of his particular teaching style, his students, and the class peer structure. Thus the question of adaptation is a complex one. See the adaptation phase of the case study of Mrs. Jefferson in Chapter Ten for an example of a teacher who worked with the many variables of teacher style, student characteristics, and classroom social structure to establish priorities for action in the adaptation of her plan.

## The Action Stage

The actual trying out of a new teaching practice presents problems of its own. A teaching practice is more than a plan; it is an integrated behavior pattern, a style of performance to be used in working with young learners that one hopes will be more effective than previous practices. This usually requires that the teacher be able to make shifts in his typical ways of thinking, that he remain flexible at all times, that he develop new behavioral skills, and that he risk behaving differently with his students from what they have come to expect. All these demands make classroom innovation a challenge, and the teacher is apt to find a variety of resistances both within himself and in the class that must be coped with if he is to successfully bridge the gap between planning and performance.

Any new procedure requires some initial practice, and this is especially true of the complex behavior patterns of teaching. Because a creative trial-and-error process is involved, various types of personal support are advisable; otherwise the risks and the inevitable partial failure that the teacher will experience in the first tryouts may result in his giving up the new ideas and concluding that they were not worthwhile. Furthermore, without practice and personal support, the new practice may be frozen at a relatively low level of quality because of the lack of flexibility in the first stages of the action-taking process.

A new technique can be practiced by oneself in front of a mirror or with a tape recorder, but very often skill and confidence can be gained only by getting the reactions of other people. One way of getting these reactions might be to interest a small group of students in staying after school to try out some new ways of organizing the class. The learning of a new technique can be made a cooperative project; the teacher can admit that he has not used it with a class before, thereby soliciting student support. The students can help not only by suggesting improvements in the teacher's method, but also by discussing possible alternative ways to deal with the problem.

Very often the teacher will want objective reaction to his early attempts to use the technique with the entire class. One effective procedure is to invite another teacher to visit the classroom and to discuss his observations soon after the classroom session. Sometimes an outside resource person such as a school psychologist, a principal, or a university educator can be invited in as a consultant.

A teacher could also make tape recordings of the early sessions and later review the tape by himself or with another teacher or a consultant. Using the tape with the students would be one method of gaining feedback from them on how they felt about the new technique and the teacher's method of implementing it.

Rapid feedback from the class is perhaps the most important means of getting guidance and support in the early stages of using a new practice in the classroom. Some feedback techniques and instruments will be described in detail in Chapter Nine.

Another way for a teacher to increase his chances for a successful tryout of a new practice is for him to share his commitment to action with one or more colleagues who have a mutual interest in the new idea or practice. Research and everyday experience have shown that a shared commitment increases the probability that action will result from an intention or decision. There are two reasons for this. One is that living up to the commitment is a strong motivating force; the other is that a group of colleagues can provide important support for each other during the early stages of a new activity. Team teaching also carries this potential for mutual support, although frequently it does not have the desired effect.

Perhaps there are two or three other teachers in a building who would also like to get the feel of a different practice and would agree to meet after school or in the evening. Some of the practices described in Chapter Seven could be tried out, with each teacher taking turns at being the teacher or one of the students. It would be ideal, of course, to secure the consultant help of some teacher who had used these practices previously and would be willing to share some of his insights. Failing this, or in addition, the advice of other resource persons might be sought.

In some schools and school systems, a university research team has held professional clinic sessions with several teachers. Most program time was spent with each teacher describing a classroom problem he had run into during the week and delineating the situation in detail up to the point of his difficulty in interaction with a student or with a class. At this point, the other members of the group quickly wrote down what they felt would be best to do at the moment. They read their suggestions to the rest of the group, and then the teacher seeking help had the option of trying out the ideas that seemed most promising to him with his colleagues playing the roles of the students.

In another type of teacher-training session, a group of teachers, working together during the summer on the improvement of their teaching techniques and the development of new curriculum practices, recruited a small team of children in the neighborhood to be available on call to come in and help them try out new teaching ideas. The students were enthusiastic about the opportunity, and the teachers benefited from being able to try out new practices in a situation similar to actual classroom conditions.

## CHAPTER NINE

# *Feedback and Evaluation*

In the last phase of the problem-solving sequence the teacher assesses the effects of his new practice both by obtaining student feedback and by carrying out an objective evaluation. These two assessment objectives are not necessarily reached by the same methods. The students may feel comfortable with a teaching practice and may approve of it; yet the teaching practice may be attractive to them because it demands no effort, and thus the learning atmosphere may not have improved. However, unless the students feel somewhat secure with the teaching practice, the learning atmosphere will still not improve. Consequently, this chapter will discuss first the ways in which the teacher can use student feedback to find out how they feel about his new practices, and then the ways in which the teacher can make objective, long-term evaluations of whether or not the learning atmosphere has improved.

## *Feedback*

Feedback from students is invaluable for the classroom teacher trying to judge the effectiveness of a new teaching practice. It is a corrective mechanism for the teacher who wants to improve his teaching practices and to learn how well his execution matches his intentions. All too often teachers view feedback as something that should proceed from teacher to student only. When they do solicit feedback from the student, it is in a forced and formal way that encourages the student to give the reaction that he thinks the teacher wants him to give. Thus the teacher may learn nothing new about his behavior and skills; he may receive only a reflection of his projected self-image.

Since the teacher is an authority figure, getting spontaneous and honest feedback from students is an art in itself. In some cases the teacher may have to invest considerable time and energy to convince his students that he wants them to be honest and that it is safe for them to be so. Students are not likely to believe him at first.

## Conducting Open Feedback Discussions

If the communications atmosphere is open and relaxed, and the students are able to freely and honestly express their feelings, the best method of gaining feedback on a new practice is to discuss the results of it with the class. By asking for their reactions and giving them feedback about their behavior, the teacher may help to focus the responsibility for constructive change on the students themselves. This procedure also may help set the stage for other practices that involve the students even more in the process of change, self-development, and growth.

Some teachers have found that it is feasible and easy for them to conduct feedback discussions at the end of their first tryout of a new approach. To get this open public feedback from the students, the teacher should explain that he is trying out a new practice, and that he would like their thoughtful reactions so that he can improve it. He should stress the fact that he thinks the practice can be improved. Thus the students will not think that the teacher will take their comments as personal attacks on him. To gain their trust, he must not allow the feedback to be a one-way process; in the discussion he should give them feedback upon their behavior. He can, for example, explain exactly why he thought it was necessary to institute the new practice, and what the students can do to make it more effective. There are several important criteria for giving and receiving feedback between teacher and students. The classroom atmosphere should be supportive, nonthreatening, and nondefensive. Feedback should be descriptive rather than evaluative; by avoiding judgmental and evaluative language, the teacher can reduce the student's need to react defensively and make rationalizations about his behavior. Furthermore, effective feedback to students should be specific rather than general so that the students know exactly what the teacher is talking about. Feedback should also be well timed; in general it is most useful if given at the earliest opportunity after the behavior in question.

A variation of the open feedback discussion is to involve only the individual students or groups of students whose behaviors and indications of feeling first provoked concern. The teacher might present or discuss the original data he collected and ask the students whether they feel there has been a change in themselves or in the classroom. The teacher might ask them how they now feel about themselves, their peers, the teacher, or their work in school.

## Building an Open Communications Atmosphere

When the atmosphere in the classroom is not free and encouraging, the teacher cannot expect much success with open discussion. He can, however, work toward improving the classroom communications atmosphere by using feedback techniques and devices that demand less of his students in the way of exposing themselves to the reactions of their peers and the teacher. The technique of student anonymity and simple mood-indicating devices are excellent for this purpose. They can be used not only to help loosen the atmosphere, but also to give the teacher valuable feedback, although the information will not be as specific and useful as open discussion in a relaxed classroom atmosphere.

Anonymous feedback can be gotten by using diagnostic questionnaires that measure student reaction to the new teaching practice. Questionnaires of this type are sometimes called postclass reactions; they are discussed in detail in Chapter Two of the booklet *Diagnosing Classroom Learning Environments*.

The following are examples of some feedback questions not included in that booklet:

How did you feel about our _____ period today?

| Not so bad | Quite good | Fairly good | Very good |
|---|---|---|---|
| _____ | _____ | _____ | _____ |

Why did you mark where you did? How could it have been better?

_____

_____

What do you think about the way the teacher led the _____ period today?

| Helped me learn a lot | Helped me learn quite a bit | Didn't help me learn much |
|---|---|---|
| _____ | _____ | _____ |

Why did you mark where you did?

_____

_____

The teacher might also ask the students about the clarity of a lesson, whether they ever felt lost during the lesson, and if they wanted extra help during the lesson. Many other questions would be possible in this context. Such simple items as the following could be useful:

What was your personal reaction to the lesson?

| Very clear | Quite clear | Unclear, vague | Very fuzzy |
|---|---|---|---|
| _____ | _____ | _____ | _____ |

— or —

How helpful was our discussion today?

| Very helpful | Somewhat helpful | Not very helpful | Not helpful at all |
|---|---|---|---|
| _____ | _____ | _____ | _____ |

The teacher can then discuss the information received from the questionnaires with the entire class. As the class begins to understand that the teacher does not feel threatened by negative feedback, and that he wants to correct any practices that adversely affect the students, they will be more ready and able to react openly and honestly. When the atmosphere has become this supportive and free, the teacher is well advised to have students put their names or preassigned numbers on their questionnaires. In this way he can identify individuals or groups that are reacting negatively to the new practice and the reasons why they do not feel comfortable with it. The regular use of diagnostic questionnaires can provide the teacher with a systematic means of receiving continuous feedback from his class that may be more effective than open class discussions. Questionnaires can be selected from *Diagnosing Classroom Learning Environments* or developed by the teacher to tap areas that might be difficult to handle in open discussion. Through the use of a series of questionnaires, the teacher can get everyone's opinion on a variety of the aspects of the new practice; he can cover more ground than would be possible in class discussion. Optimal procedures for obtaining feedback combine open discussion with these questionnaires.

Simple mood-indicating devices can also be used to improve the classroom atmosphere, while at the same time providing the teacher with feedback. The advantage of these devices is that they require little initiative from the student; they give him a ready-made means of expression by asking him to respond to a simple dichotomy or series of moods that the teacher has provided in advance. In other words, these devices minimize the barriers to student reaction.

An example of such a device is a mood barometer, which is like a thermometer with indices of feelings. It might be constructed of a round piece of cardboard with a metal arrow that can be moved around the circle and pointed in any direction. The piece of cardboard is divided into pie segments and each segment is labeled with a feeling, such as "feel great," "can't stand it," "very comfortable." Each pupil could have one of these on his desk and might turn the arrow in the direction he feels at any given time. Another use that might be made of such a barometer is for the teacher to have one on his desk and to indicate to the students how he feels from time to time. A similar device, especially relevant for a class of very young children, is a group of several small puppets that the teacher can keep on his desk to show the students how he thinks they feel. The students thus learn that feelings can be expressed through the puppets. The teacher might later place these puppets at strategic points in the room so that the students themselves can show how they feel.

As another device, the teacher might use three small cardboard boxes, each with a face on it indicating pleasure, neutrality, or displeasure. The faces should be very simple: smiling, impassive, and frowning. Each student would be asked to select the face that best reflected his feelings

71

about the day's work. Before they leave the classroom at lunchtime or at the end of the day, the teacher might place these three boxes on his desk, or on a table at the front of the room, next to a basket of beads, a package of pins, or several slips of paper. On his way out each student would pick up a bead, pin, or slip and drop it in the box that expressed his feelings about the day.

With all these devices the teacher will want to discuss the results with the class. After the students have heard the teacher commenting nonpunitively and constructively upon both the negative and positive feedbacks received from the devices, they will feel more secure about expressing their feelings openly and honestly.

Once the classroom atmosphere has become more open through the use of anonymous questionnaires and mood-indicating devices, the teacher is advised to use class discussion to gain more spontaneous and rapid feedback from students. He can do this and still provide the security of some degree of anonymity through several discussion methods. One method that relieves the discussion participants of the burden of taking direct responsibility for their expressed opinions is role playing. The teacher can pick a half dozen or so youngsters to play the roles of "typical students." He could assign them fictitious names to further separate them from the feeling of personal responsibility for their reactions. For the role-playing situation, he would ask them to pretend that they were in the school lunchroom, or on the playground, or in a school hangout, talking about the new teaching practice. The interested teacher should refer to the booklet *Role-Playing Methods in the Classroom* for further discussion of the many ways role playing can be used to stimulate students to express their feelings.

Another discussion technique that preserves student anonymity is the division of the class into "buzz" groups of four or five students each. These groups can meet separately to discuss the teaching practice; they provide a relatively safe setting in which the individual student can express both negative and positive reactions. One member of each group is then selected or elected to present the views of the entire group to the class. The views are presented as coming from the entire group; thus the negative or positive reactions of each individual are not revealed to the teacher or to most of his classmates.

Yet even when the youngsters have been convinced that the teacher desires that they tell him their feelings, they will usually still need substantial instruction and support in expressing feelings in constructive ways. They may not be sure how to help, even when they wish to. The teacher can set up role-playing demonstrations in which positive and negative forms of feedback are demonstrated and the various ways of giving critical feedback are explored.

72

A final cautionary note to the teacher who is trying to build an open communications atmosphere in his class is needed. In his solicitude to appear permissive so that the students will react honestly and freely, he may make the mistake of allowing the feedback process to become unilateral, with the students offering their honest reactions and the teacher dissimulating his. The students will soon catch on, and they may believe that they are being tricked into incriminating themselves; thus they too will dissemble their honest reactions. Of course the teacher should exercise care and tact in giving feedback to students, remembering to be descriptive rather than evaluative, specific rather than general, and timely rather than too late with his comments.

## An Example of a Continuous Feedback Procedure

A regular procedure for exchanging feedback was employed by Mr. Elston's sixth-grade class. About every two or three weeks the students filled out a teacher "feedback sheet" in which they would each check a number of scales to show how they saw their teacher's actions. Then they would draw a line to the place on the scale indicating how they wanted him to be. For example:

Amount of Freedom to Do Things on Our Own

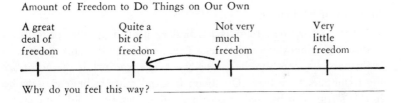

Why do you feel this way? _____

While the students were filling out their scales, Mr. Elston would fill out a series of scales indicating how he saw the class and how he wanted them to be. For example:

Amount of Student Responsibility for Asking and for Giving Help to Each Other

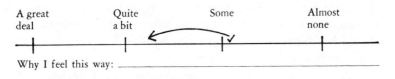

Why I feel this way: _____

A classroom committee summarized the data from the student questionnaires, putting it up on the board along with the data from Mr. Elston's ratings. The teacher and students then discussed the feedback received

73

from each other and ways it could guide them in improving the learning activities and teacher-student relations in their classroom. Both the students and the teacher were enthusiastic about the improvement in their working relationship as the result of this two-way feedback and discussion procedure.

## Evaluation

During the evaluation phase, as in the diagnostic phase, the teacher again is interested in obtaining data on student characteristics, classroom social patterns, and teacher-student relations. However, he now wants to learn whether his innovative practices have changed the classroom climate in any way. Casual observation of classroom activity is not enough. Careful and forthright evaluation may uncover what are really unhealthy aspects of even the most disciplined, quiet, and well-mannered classroom group. It is easy for the teacher to deceive himself. Often, because of his legitimate desire to do a good job, he may see changes where there are none; just as easily, he may see no progress where a great deal of subtle change has taken place.

### Methods of Evaluation

The teacher's objectivity is a critical element in his attempt to validly evaluate his innovative practices. The more objective his method of evaluation, the more sure he can be about how worthwhile the new teaching techniques have been. Questionnaires and other techniques described in this section can be used to obtain a certain degree of objective evaluation.

Getting measures both early and late in the problem-solving process should enable the teacher to make a clear assessment of classroom change. In an ideal situation the teacher can use the very same assessment tool in both the diagnostic and evaluative phases. For example, he might readminister a sociometric device that was utilized during the diagnostic stage, analyze and interpret the results, and finally compare these with the results from the first administration. If students have changed their interpersonal feelings and if the peer group social structure has altered, the teacher might be able to point to his own problem-solving activity as the genesis of this improvement.

Yet even though the classroom situation may have improved, the teacher cannot be sure that the improvement was caused by his teaching innovation. It may have improved for other reasons. Just as forces in the community can adversely influence a youngster's attitude toward school, other community forces may operate to improve it. An example may be the case of change in school attitudes of peer leaders due to a social worker's particular success with a gang of these students.

Although the teacher will be happy to see an improvement, as a professional he will want to know what effect his teaching practices have had on the change. His evaluation is not only concerned with the classroom situation; it is also concerned with his new teaching practice. He might make an additional check by comparing two subgroups of pupils, one in which he has attempted some new technique and the other in which he has not made such efforts. If these two groups scored roughly the same on the initial administration of the diagnostic instrument, differences between the groups' responses on the later administration may indicate the effectiveness of the teacher's actions. This procedure might involve readministering a parental attitude and influence questionnaire and then comparing the answers of two subgroups of pupils. With one group the teacher might have used role playing to help them understand their perceptions of their parents' attitudes toward school and the effect these perceptions have upon their academic performance; the other group might have been working on other projects while the role-playing sessions were taking place. An analysis should follow in which the teacher determines whether there is any difference and, if so, in what direction. In this way he may discover whether the role-playing sessions might be responsible for any positive changes in the students' ability to cope with parental attitudes toward academic efforts. This general procedure is similar to the controlled experiment, which is prevalent in the scientific designs of social research.

Another evaluation technique is for the teacher to bring in a colleague or consultant to observe him while teaching. This is most effective when the original classroom situation was diagnosed with the aid of such an observer, as discussed in Chapter Four.

Another technique that can be particularly effective, if handled properly by the teacher, is to hold interviews with individual students. He should interview those students whose behavior seems to have undergone a change. He should be careful that his questions do not show the student that a certain answer is expected; otherwise the student may merely say what he thinks the teacher wants to be told. Sample approaches to use in a semistructured interview of this type would be as follows: "I notice that you seem to be much more interested in what is going on in class these days. Why do you think that happened?" "I notice that your homework assignments are much better now. Can you tell me anything about that?" If the student mentions the new teaching practice, the teacher should be careful to direct further discussion as little as possible. He might ask, "Why do you think the new practice makes any difference in the way you do your homework?" This interview technique might not work if there has been extensive class discussion of the teaching practice beforehand or if the teacher has explained his goals to the whole class, for the value of the interview lies greatly in the student's not thinking that there are any "right" answers to these questions.

### Results of Evaluation

The teacher may discover that the classroom situation has substantially improved; yet the solution of one set of problems often brings other problems into the open. For example, if he has successfully changed the classroom social structure from a hierarchical one to a more diffused one, he can expect new problems in leadership to arise, much on the analogy of a country that replaces a dictatorship with a democracy.

In other cases, if the teacher had discovered a number of problems in the diagnostic phase that had to be dealt with separately and sequentially, the solution of one problem now frees him to deal with another.

If his evaluation shows that his teaching innovation failed completely in its purpose or had very little effect, the teacher will want to review the phases in the problem-solving sequence to see whether the fault lay in the problem identification, diagnosis, plan development, adaptation and execution, or feedback. He may decide that he had a good plan but that he did not adapt it properly to his situation. Or he may decide that the classroom problems need a rediagnosis.

If evaluation shows that the problem has been only partially remedied, he may be able to use his partial success as a foundation on which to build further change efforts. For example, a teacher who wanted to stimulate student participation in learning through small work-project groups may learn that the groups were a failure because of the intense competition for power within each group. Reflection on this evaluation may show that this competitiveness can be used to increase learning. He might, for example, decide to modify his plan by having each student work individually within his group, and reward the most productive student in each group each week by making that student the group chairman with duties such as keeping daily records of the productivity of the other members, or of being the liaison agent between the group and the teacher so that other members would have to go through the chairman to ask help from the teacher.

The final result of the evaluation stage should be to show the teacher what problems have been solved and to what extent; what problems remain to be solved; what new problems the teaching innovation has caused; what successes he can use in further innovation efforts; and so forth. In this sense, evaluation is a rediagnosis that leads to new plan development, adaptation, execution, feedback, and evaluation again. Problem solving in the classroom is a never ending process.

CHAPTER TEN

# Four Case Studies

This chapter will present the experiences of three teachers who used this problem-solving process to improve their classroom learning climates. The first two case studies will deal with classrooms described in Chapter One, the third with a classroom described in Chapter Six. The last case study is of a school system's efforts to facilitate the sharing of ideas among its teachers.

## Mrs. Jefferson's Secondary School Classroom

### Phase 1: Identifying the Classroom Problems

The difficulties that Mrs. Jefferson was having with her class were introduced in Chapter One. She knew that she did a conscientious job of maintaining discipline and that her teaching style appealed to some of her students who were highly involved in their studies. However, her class seemed overly dependent on her for guidance, direction, and motivation; and she knew that there were many students to whom her teaching style did not appeal. Even the highly involved students seldom introduced new and different topics representing their own concerns into the classroom discussions. Her tentative identification of the problem was that it was primarily one of a lack of rapport between teacher and students. This situation was possibly caused by her style of teaching, by student misconceptions of their own roles, or by student reluctance to show academic enthusiasm in front of their peers and the teacher.

### Phase 2: Diagnosing the Classroom Problems

Mrs. Jefferson decided to try to ascertain the causes of this apathy and general lack of creativity in learning. She constructed a series of questions focusing on student interests and the relations between students and teachers. Through the use of this questionnaire she found that her students thought that all classroom planning should be the task of the teacher, and that the proper student role was the passive absorption of content. As a result of this outlook, students depended on Mrs. Jefferson to initiate and maintain their interest in academic tasks. Furthermore, the questionnaire results showed that the students generally felt quite negatively about learning tasks. The students also revealed that they felt that they should not help one another with academic tasks.

## Phase 3:   Developing a Plan

With such diagnostic information, Mrs. Jefferson incorporated three approaches to the difficulty in a single plan: (1) student planning, (2) student grouping on the basis of whom the class members thought they could best work with, and (3) student teaching. By encouraging student planning, Mrs. Jefferson wanted to give the class some responsibility for determining and planning the lessons to be taught and the issues to be covered. Student grouping procedures would be devised to diminish the impersonality of her class and to engage students with one another in small, compatible work groups that might lead to shared enthusiasm about academic projects. Finally, with student teaching Mrs. Jefferson desired to have students make up the lessons on specific topics and actually teach them to the class. In this way she hoped that they would do more than their usual amount of work in preparation for classroom presentation, become involved and committed to their individual or group projects, and learn to use one another as valuable resources. She established an order of priority, realizing that all three plans could not be put into operation at the same time. With the present authoritarian-dependent classroom atmosphere, she could not hope for much success with student planning and teaching. The students would be overly dependent upon her for advice; some of the more involved students would merely plan and teach as they thought Mrs. Jefferson would do it, and the other pupils would be apathetic to and resentful of the extra energy such tasks called for. Therefore she gave priority to the raising of student initiative and enthusiasm, and she thought this could best be done through the formation of small work-project groups.

## Phase 4:   Adaptation and Action

On the basis of this general plan for solving problems of student involvement, Mrs. Jefferson proceeded in the following way. First, she discussed with the entire class the possibility of forming small study groups. Because her students had negative attitudes about working together, she thought she could generate more enthusiasm at first by permitting them to choose their own groups. After the students seemed to understand the benefits of cooperation, she reorganized the groups so that the students would gain varied experience in working with others.

The second step in her approach was outlining to the groups, and particularly to group leaders, what their jobs and special responsibilities were. She stressed the importance of leadership responsibility because of long-standing habits of student passivity and dependence. After several weeks in which the students became accustomed to working in groups with minimal supervision, Mrs. Jefferson invited interested groups to submit lesson plans covering a two-week unit of work. Of course she clearly maintained responsibility for advising and editing all suggestions, because she realized that she too had long-standing classroom habits and would not be comfortable if she gave too much autonomy to her students. The students understood that their lesson plans were suggested outlines for the entire class to follow and that Mrs. Jefferson would select from this list several that she approved of. From this edited list the teacher drew up a master plan of ideas and distributed it to all the working groups. Each group then voted on the plans and programs on which they wanted to work. The responsibility for selecting the curriculum and for organizing and teaching it was thus transferred to the small student groups.

Mrs. Jefferson realized that there was still the danger of each group falling into a pattern similar to that exhibited by the whole class; that is, with one or two highly involved students doing all the work and the others sitting by, bored and resentful. Therefore she stipulated that the group as a whole present its lesson to the class so that each member would be involved in the presentation. In this way she further reinforced habits of cooperation among the students.

### Phase 5:  Feedback and Evaluation

Mrs. Jefferson had no trouble getting relatively indirect and continuous feedback from her students on their reactions to the new classroom practice. Because of the students' habits of dependency, they were constantly asking her for advice. She recognized that these requests were often barely concealed complaints about the difficulty of working with the other members of the group. At times the complaints were quite open. Gradually, however, as the groups got closer to the formation of plans and the execution of them, she noticed that their requests for advice were more on matters of procedure and substance. Also the requests began to come from the groups as cohesive entities rather than from frustrated individuals. This gradual and subtle change in the nature of student dependency was sufficient feedback to her plans.

Because of this feedback and the apparent change in her students' ability to work together without her constant attention, Mrs. Jefferson liked the procedure. Although she made no systematic evaluation of it, she decided to use it again the following year. Reflection on her experience made her realize that she preferred to assign students to groups herself because it permitted her to place certain rejected students with highly accepted and competent ones. She hoped that the isolated and rejected students might be able to learn new interpersonal skills by working with more socially effective peers. When the students worked out their own groups they generally chose their own friends, and most of the rejected youngsters were left in a group by themselves. Thus they were in a poor position to learn new skills.

In either grouping system, Mrs. Jefferson felt she had effectively transferred responsibility for learning, and even for some teaching, to the students in her class. She felt that because of this increased student responsibility, her students now had a higher motivation to participate in class and learn the academic materials. Instead of just absorbing materials she presented, they actively concerned themselves with learning.

## Mr. Jackson's Intermediate School Classroom

### Phases 1 and 2:   Identifying and Diagnosing the Classroom Problems

The situation in Mr. Jackson's classroom was discussed and illustrated in Chapter One. He was aware of difficulties in interpersonal and intergroup relations among his students as evidenced by expressions of ambivalence, intolerance, and hostility. He saw, as possible sources of the problem, community attitudes that conditioned students to reject the importance and value of individual and group differences. Classroom learning and attention to academic tasks clearly suffered as a result of these antagonistic peer relations. There were probably many reasons for these antagonisms, but clearly the major issues were interracial and intersocial-class distrust. Before he could work on any other classroom problem, Mr. Jackson had to deal with these major issues.

### Phase 3:   Developing a Plan

Mr. Jackson met with several colleagues in the school to discuss his problem. Since the neighborhood was changing, other teachers encountered similar incidents and difficulties in their classes. They shared several ideas for dealing with the situation and decided that an effective plan had to meet two conditions: (1) contributing to the security of individual students, since the insecurity of the student who perceives himself rejected by the group or others hampers that individual's learning; and (2) improving relations between subgroups within the class, thereby contributing to the learning efficiency of the whole class.

Mr. Jackson and his colleagues developed a variety of tentative approaches, including the following:

1. The use of role playing to develop appreciation of problems of new and different students.
2. The use of data from the preceding year's class (without identifying it as such) to point out attitudes toward classwork and classmates and to derive specific questions to be used in class group discussions—for example:

   "How can you feel self-confident without having people think you're stuck up?"

   "How do students in this class feel about the class?"

   "Why do youngsters think that teachers and principals have a lower opinion of them than their parents? Do they?"

   "Do youngsters get a fixed notion as to how teachers and principals are supposed to feel, and see them this way regardless of the way they act? Do we do this with other people?"
3. Studying about people (especially teen-agers) in other lands in order to observe differences in standards of behavior and appearance.
4. The use of a class newspaper to increase recognition of the importance and contributions of all those who are in school.
5. Dividing the class into small heterogeneous groups to consider problems of individual adjustment and group relations.
6. The development of simple diagrams of concepts of "life space" and "force fields" to increase the students' ability to perceive and appreciate differences.
7. Giving small interracial peer groups increased responsibility for planning and carrying out learning activities in the classroom.
8. The use of common interests as a basis for grouping or regrouping.
9. The use of a questionnaire on classroom jobs once a month to encourage recognition and appreciation of various abilities, and to encourage additional breadth of experience for all class members.
10. Studying about prejudice and stereotyping as a natural phenomenon that may cause problems and can be controlled, even in the classroom.
11. Having small groups study and teach the rest of the class about current events.

Mr. Jackson decided to concentrate on two major practices, each partly derived from the above list: (1) teaching students how to work effectively in task-oriented groups; and (2) using common-interest groups to study, plan, and present materials on current social problems in the class. These

81

two approaches seem most appropriate for the priorities he established while thinking about the problem. He felt that if students understood how groups do and can work together, they might improve group cohesiveness, group satisfaction, and respect and acceptance for individual members, and gain skill in formulating and accomplishing their objectives. Furthermore, successful cross-race group work would help break down some of the barriers to communication and friendship, and grouping students on the basis of common interest would probably ensure formation of cross-race groups.

## Phase 4: Adaptation and Action

The class began by talking as a whole about some of the things that help or hinder a small group's work. Such dimensions as bossiness, different goals, nonsharing of attention, rejection of individuals, and apathy were submitted by the students. Mr. Jackson established a series of role-playing situations to demonstrate some of these interpersonal styles and their effect on group work. Mr. Jackson asked five pupils to role-play a group at work. One of these group members was asked to behave very bossily and two others were asked to disagree vehemently. This role-play situation successfully dramatized some of the problems students encountered in working together. After the class had discussed this dramatic and realistic example, several other students role-played the activities of a group with less obvious conflicts. Through repeated role playing and discussion, each of the major barriers to effective group work was highlighted and examined; then alternative resolutions were discussed. Finally Mr. Jackson and his class were able to establish a list of principles for effective group work. These principles were put up on the wall for all students to see and refer to during their work together. The list was as follows:

1. It helps to listen to one another.
2. It helps to find out what others are thinking.
3. It helps to give others some attention.
4. Everyone needs to feel a part of things.
5. It helps if everyone has a say in decisions.
6. It helps to remember Mr. Jackson is in no hurry for us to finish.

Perhaps the most important feature of this beginning list was that the students and Mr. Jackson constructed it together; it had meaning for the students in terms of their own experience, and not merely as a series of abstract dicta from the teacher.

Mr. Jackson began the second part of his plan by talking with his students about important social and community problems. After a brief overview of social problems, some lectures on selected topics, and individual reading, groups of students decided which issue or topic they felt was most important to them. These groups were formed on the basis of individuals' common interests, and their membership included students of both races. Students were then encouraged to read more about these problems in current periodicals and newspapers and do original research into their causes and effects. Since current material was not always simple to find, and since some students were unsure about their ability to work in groups, Mr. Jackson met with each group, serving as a catalyst and helping the groups plan their activities. In some cases he spent most of his time attending to group problems in working together. In other cases his major contribution took the form of assisting in locating materials, or showing students where and how to find things.

The next step was for each small group to plan and present a panel discussion to the entire class. Some student groups prepared visual materials such as movies or charts and arranged for speakers such as ministers, police officers, and other community leaders. The panel discussion period was followed by a general discussion on each topic by the class as a whole. This discussion served to add others' knowledge and points of view and to evaluate the effectiveness of the small group's presentation. Whenever students became overly critical of an individual's or a group's contribution, Mr. Jackson indicated and enforced the standard that the evaluation should be helpful to the individual or the group.

### Phase 5:   Feedback and Evaluation

The fact that the working groups had been so successful was important feedback for Mr. Jackson. He felt that this indicated they understood some of the problems of working with others and had gained a growing intellectual understanding of and involvement in such problems as juvenile delinquency and racial integration. This awareness in young people is the first step toward solution of the classroom manifestations of community and social issues. Furthermore, the small groups seemed to have a sense of accomplishment and pride when they felt they had completed a worthwhile project of their own. New working relations along interest and task lines, instead of clearly racial lines, began to occur and inhere in the class. Mr. Jackson felt he and his class had taken some important steps toward solving these community and classroom problems of intergroup and interpersonal relations.


## Mrs. Dome's Second-Grade Classroom

Since the first three phases of Mrs. Dome's problem-solving process were described fully in Chapter Six, they will be only briefly summarized here. The fourth and fifth phases will be presented in detail.

### Phases 1 and 2:   Identifying and Diagnosing the Classroom Problems

Mrs. Dome's students did not get along well with one another; they often fought on the school grounds and argued in class. Most of the fighting seemed to be confined to a few students who did not appear to have many friends in the class. These fighters seldom played with the other students and often seemed bored and withdrawn from games and activities. When at certain times they did ask to play, the other children refused their request. Mrs. Dome administered a sociometric test that asked students whom they liked being with, whom they liked to play with and work with, and whom they didn't like being with. The test results showed there were a few highly chosen and well-liked children, and a few who were often rejected. In addition, a cyclical process of peer rejection, frustration, and aggression further isolated the socially ineffective students.

### Phase 3:   Developing a Plan

Mrs. Dome decided to try several different plans to change her classroom situation. One plan called for special responsibility training for socially effective and popular students and special support sessions for rejected students. Another plan developed out of her interest in the auxiliary chair technique as a means of dramatizing and stimulating discussion of peer behavior patterns.

Finally, she decided to help her students learn about social interaction by observing younger students and by studying the behavioral sciences.

### Phase 4:   Adaptation and Action

Mrs. Dome modified the auxiliary chair technique to make it relevant to the age of her students and to the problems of her group. In dealing with a problem of physical aggression and the events leading up to it, for instance, Mrs. Dome put the chair on her desk for all to see and announced that the chair's name was Tuffy. First she asked the class to describe how a "Tuffy" behaves. She then said that Tuffy had just asked to play with someone and had been refused. She asked the class to tell how they thought Tuffy felt. In this way all the students could participate in the projection of their feelings onto Tuffy without worrying about hurting anyone in particular. After students had volunteered this information, Mrs. Dome asked how Tuffy could have managed to ask to play in such a way as not to be refused. Then the chair was shifted to another role, the role of Noplay, the type of person who refused to let Tuffy play, and the class responded to Mrs. Dome's request to tell how else Noplay might have behaved in this situation. They offered some suggestions to Noplay as to how he might have acted so as not to provoke Tuffy's resentment and aggression.

Mrs. Dome also tried some special training sessions for her students to see younger students at work. But since children in kindergarten seldom work on subject matter for long intervals, she decided to modify her plan to include observations of older, more academically involved students. Mrs. Dome solicited the help of teachers of the third and fourth grades. These teachers agreed to try the chair technique in their classes and to have Mrs. Dome's students observe. Mrs. Dome's students observed and listened to their elders' comments about why people are aggressive, loud, quiet, or shy, and how one might help them. In some cases the older children were much more effective than Mrs. Dome could have been in reaching her students, and they represented more positive models than the kindergarten youngsters.

Mrs. Dome felt that these occasional insights were not sufficient and needed to be supplemented by formal and continual training. She decided to hold a weekly lesson period on human relations and behavioral science. She had originally planned to start out with a lesson on working in small groups, but decided instead on one on expressing positive and negative feelings because this was so closely associated with her auxiliary chair practice. Later in the year, after the students had gotten accustomed to these units, she integrated them more into her subject-matter concerns. The unit on working in small groups was done at the same time groups were formed to work on social studies projects.

## Phase 5: Feedback and Evaluation

Through the use of the auxiliary chair as the prototype of many kinds of social behaviors, the students began to be able to identify the kinds of behaviors that would create resentment on the part of the Noplays and the Tuffies. They understood how the interaction between Tuffy and Noplay was a combination of the feelings of both. In the more immediate sense, students began to be able to empathize with their peers. They were ready to assume some responsibility for the training of their peers, for the acceptance of individual differences in skill and style, and for the patience to deal with their Tuffy and Noplay companions. At the same time, the previously rejected students were now willing to accept the overtures of their peer leaders.

Through the laboratory study of selected problems in social relations, the students began to gain skills in systematically observing and changing their own behavior and that of their peers.

At the conclusion of the school year Mrs. Dome attempted an objective evaluation of the interpersonal situation in her classroom. She had noticed many changes—among them, fewer fights—but wished to weigh her own preceptions against her students' actual attitudes and feelings. She used the same sociometric instrument she administered in the beginning of the semester. She also presented the students with some descriptions of common interpersonal situations and asked them to identify the feelings of each of the participants. For instance, she constructed the story that John had just pushed Joan on the playground after John's friends laughed at him for walking with Joan. Then she asked the students to write or tell what they thought John was thinking and feeling, what Joan was thinking and feeling, and what John's friends thought and felt.

The results of this evaluation procedure convinced Mrs. Dome that her innovations had been successful in many ways. In the first place, the number of rejected students had diminished considerably. There seemed to be a greater diffusion of positive choices, so that fewer pupils were very highly liked or very strongly rejected. Furthermore, she observed less fighting in the schoolyard, and all her students played and worked together more often. Students who still disliked some of their peers were nevertheless now able to work with them without overt hostility. Finally, the responses to the problem situations she constructed showed outstanding empathy and understanding. She felt that her students were far more sophisticated than comparable second-graders whom she had taught but who had not received such special training. Student leaders were ready and able to take more responsibility for helping the socially handicapped members of the class. The previously rejected students were getting help in learning socially acceptable behavior patterns. Her work also indicated that the classroom can be used as a laboratory for teaching behavioral standards, social responsibility, and behavioral science concepts.

Mrs. Dome indicated that she would make a few changes in the practices for the next school year. Specifically, she wished to make greater use of role-playing techniques in the early sessions where she had used only the auxiliary chair. One of the reasons she had not used role playing earlier was her lack of acquaintance with this procedure. Now that she was more comfortable using it, she thought she would like to introduce it earlier. Furthermore, she felt that she would like to give the fourth- and sixth-graders who came and helped her some special training in how to work with younger children. Finally, she felt she would like to talk about some of her innovations with the other teachers in the school. She believed that her problems and solutions were not unique, except perhaps in timing and combination, and that other teachers might be more willing to try such innovations if they knew they had been used successfully.

## Albertson School System Facilitates the Sharing of Plans

A resource pool of teaching plans could be a great help to the teacher who has identified and diagnosed the problems in his own classroom but needs help in planning a course of action. In this example a systemwide committee of classroom teachers, working with the administration and with a scientist consultant, planned a practice-sharing day. All classes were canceled for that day and most of the teachers in the school system attended the sessions. The elementary and secondary classroom teachers met with the administrators in a half-hour general session at which they received a briefing by the consultant on how diffusion and sharing of new practices have been developed in other fields, such as agriculture and medicine, and some of the particular problems that educators have in sharing professional practices. The teachers then broke into grade-level discussion groups, with the administrators meeting as a separate group. A guide sheet distributed to everyone suggested that the groups discuss factors inhibiting or making difficult the sharing of professional practices—factors related both to asking for help and to giving help. A recorder in each group wrote directly on ditto masters so that the findings could be available to all groups within an hour after the discussion concluded.

After lunch the participants returned to the grade-level groups with another discussion guide that directed them to make a quick census of teaching practices that the various members of the group felt might be worth sharing. From the census the group was to select a maximum of four practices to explore systematically during the afternoon. The guide sheet included a suggested set of questions that the group might want to use to get a full and concrete description of each of the four practices, and the recorder in each group had a prepared outline sheet for recording the description of each practice. Thus the descriptions could be written up and shared as a part of the record of the conference. The outline for discussing practices follows.

I. Description
   A. Please describe the teaching practice.
   B. What resources (colleagues, reading materials, etc.) did you use in developing this idea?
   C. What goals were you working toward with this practice?
   D. How did you prepare the students for the new practice?
   E. Were any special diagnostic tools or visual aids used? Please describe.
   F. What teaching methods did you use?
   G. What kinds of experiences did you hope the students would have?
   H. What happened while you were trying the new practice?

II. Evaluation
   A. From your point of view, how successful was the practice in terms of
      1. student academic learning?
      2. student mental health?
      3. your own comfort and feelings of effectiveness?
   B. How did you evaluate the outcome or success of this practice?
   C. Did some aspects of the practice work better than others? Please explain.
   D. Did some aspects work less well than others? Please explain.
   E. Would you make any change if you were to try this practice again?
III. Documentation
   Are there any activities, visual aids, special materials, or teacher-made tests we could
                        Yes    No    What?
   A. observe?
   B. take pictures of?
   C. tape or record?
   D. make copies of?
IV. Special considerations (if not mentioned above)
   A. Was it necessary to change your usual way of organizing, managing, or disciplining the class? Please explain.
   B. Could you suggest ways of increasing the effectiveness of the practice through cooperating with other teachers and classrooms?
   C. What special skills, resources, experiences, etc., would be helpful for a teacher to have to make best use of this practice?
   D. What pitfalls should a teacher be careful to avoid?

Some important aspects of this daylong session were that the procedures that were utilized sensitized the participants to the problems of communication; legitimized an active, nondefensive process of communicating; and provided the tools to help the teachers do a disciplined job of questioning a colleague about his teaching practice. This at least makes it possible for each educator to receive enough concrete information to know whether another teacher's practice is relevant to his own classroom problems and whether it seems worth considering in addition to his own repertoire of professional resources. Usually such communication does not provide enough information to permit moving into action; however, it does provide the basis for knowing whether one wants to explore further and plan some tryout efforts. The teachers would next have to make decisions about the relevance of these plans for their classroom and think about the adaptations that would be needed for them to work effectively.